IOWA PARABLES

Jerry L. Schmalenberger

FAIRWAY PRESS

DRAWER L • LIMA, OHIO 45802

IOWA PARABLES

FIRST EDITION
Copyright © 1983 by
St. John's Lutheran Church
Sixth and Keo Way
Des Moines, Iowa

•

[Bracketed material] may be adapted for local use.

7523/ISBN 0-89536-970-2   PRINTED IN U.S.A. BY FAIRWAY PRESS

TABLE OF CONTENTS

ACKNOWLEDGMENTS

A very special thanks to my secretary and typist, Susan Nedved, who carefully and quickly turned the spoken word from the transcriber into the printed word of the manuscript.

My wife, Carol, accompanied me on the many trips across Iowa, and diligently searched through historical society, newspaper, and library accounts of these stories.

Mr. William Brown of the Iowa State Historical department was also very helpful in my research.

Phil Hardee provided much of the information on the "Hidden Treasure of Siam" segment.

The Reverend John W. Christy contributed to the story about "The Little Brown Church."

Don Brown, author of *Tell a Tale of Iowa*, gave excellent support in the whole project.

George Preston of Belle Plaine, Iowa, provided historical background for the "Gusher" story.

John D. Shelley gave me material on Kate Shelley.

Veronica Keasling of Imogene, Iowa, helped with the August Werner story.

The "Plough in the Oak Tree" information came from Mrs. Wesley Foss of Exira, Iowa.

And to the many clerks and employees of the local county historical associations, I want to voice my sincere appreciation.

Now enjoy the parables.

Carol and Jerry Schmalenberger at grave site of Kate Shelley.

FOREWORD

This book is a series of sermons which recall the famous folk heroes and heroines, the events in history, that have been told from one generation to another here in Iowa. Most of the stories are related in a little book by Don Brown called *Tell a Tale of Iowa.* My wife and I have traveled to all the areas where these stories took place, searched through the historical museums, rummaged through genealogical records, waded creeks, walked fields, hunted launching and landing sites, probed for bridge piers, and interviewed relatives. We have taken slides and invaded court records, dug through old newspapers in back rooms, and braved the hostilities of unsympathetic farmers.

The reason I brought these Iowa stories to the pulpit of St. John's Lutheran Church is simple: Jesus used such local parables in His ministry to illustrate the great religious truths of His day. We still remember them and learn from them:

The Good Samaritan,
The Prodigal Son,
The Sower and the Soil,
The Lost Sheep,
The Rich Man and Lazarus,

and many more, presented by the Gospel writers who heard and retold them.

I tell them, too, because there is a certain fascination which comes in the reliving of a story. It comes especially with a story of our own land and kind of people.

I started the whole project in order to get my roots deep in Iowa soil so I could be much more effective in my pulpit as one among other Iowans. It has evolved as a way to bring the Gospel of Christ — the Good News of God — right to earth. That is, to locate the faith in our day, our home, and our neighborhood.

I considered naming the whole series "Real People" or "That's Incredible," for the stories are as true as my research can make them, and the events are, indeed, incredible!

The word "parable" in the Bible means "to lay alongside of" . . . a great truth and to illustrate it.

Matthew wrote of Jesus: "He used parables to tell them many things." (Matthew 3:3) "Then the disciples came to Jesus and asked him, 'Why do you use parables when you talk to the people?' Jesus answered, 'The knowledge about the secrets of the Kingdom of Heaven has been given to you . . . The reason I use parables in talking to them is that they look, but do not see, and they listen, but do not hear or understand. I assure you that many prophets and many of God's people wanted very much to see what you see, but they could not, and to hear what you hear, but they did not.' " (Matthew 3:3, 10, 11, 13, 17)

These parables hopefully, then, will serve as windows through which we can see clearly how God is and how He wants us to be and how we are to treat each other.

Come along with me for the stories and events which are precious and meaningful to us who live on the gentle rolling plains of Iowa.

Sincerely,
Dr. Jerry L. Schmalenberger
Senior Pastor
St. John's Lutheran Church
Des Moines, Iowa

CHAPTER 1

Kate Shelley,
Boone County Heroine

Suggested Scriptures:
Isaiah 6:1-8
Acts 20:19-24
Luke 8:22-25

Suggested Hymn:
"Lead On, O King Eternal!"

Kate Shelley Memorial Bridge

Let's go first to a little cottage up the valley of Honey Creek about half a mile from the Des Moines River. It was in Boone County, July 6, 1881.

The rain was coming down in sheets. Kate Shelley, 15, and her brothers and sisters watched the flooding river. They were very concerned that the Chicago and Northwestern railroad bridge could not hold against the flood of water, logs, and trees coming down the raging stream.

Kate's father, M. J. Shelley, an immigrant from Ireland, had been a section foreman on the railroad before he died, so his family knew well the dangers of that night.

Kate braved the rain to let out some horses and cows to take care of themselves and go for higher ground. Then she rescued some little pigs which had climbed up on a pile of hay for safety.

Later, after 11 p.m., she heard the rumble of a train — it was the "pusher," a switch engine, stationed at Moingona. It crashed into Honey Creek.

Kate decided she must help the crew and stop the passenger train — the midnight express from the West. So she started out, lantern in hand, into the frightful night to do her duty as she saw it. Unable to give aid to the ill-fated crew and knowing the midnight train was soon due, she headed west toward Moingona in an effort to save the lives of passengers.

She had to cross the railroad bridge over the Des Moines River — to attempt this in the black of this night was a scary exploit.

Kate dropped to her knees and began crawling on all fours across the long wind-swept tressel. She felt her way from tie to tie. A flash of lightning revealed an enormous uprooted tree coming down the river. Its limbs slapped her and the water ran over her as she held on for dear life.

At last she felt the solid ground beneath her feet. She got her breath and then ran to the station half a mile away.

The agent recognized her and the importance of her message. The whistle of an engine in the yards aroused the town and called men with ropes who went to the rescue of the engine-wrecked crew. Kate went with them to show them the way.

Later Kate's exploits became well-known, and she became the famous heroine of Boone County. In 1903 she accepted employment as station agent at Moingona — a position she held for nine years until her death.

Here is a real heroine, someone who put her own safety aside for the care of others. A fifteen-year-old Iowa woman, Kate, who faced terrible danger and challenge and won out — our kind of person.

This parable has something to say to us, because it's all about courage and mission.

We Christians have help in overcoming our fears.

The angels announced to the shepherds the birth of Jesus, that is, the very first words that God said to us humans upon the birth of His Son into our world were, "Fear not, don't be afraid, I'm here with good news for you, which will bring great joy to all the people." (Luke 2:10)

So we have a presence of God with us when we face frightening times. When danger faces us and when fears gnaw away at the pit of our stomach, we have courage and a bravery that helps us overcome and win and conquer.

I don't know about Kate Shelley's Christian faith, but I do know there is great courage available to us if we take God's promise and presence seriously. I'm confident, that night as she crawled from tie to tie across that rain-swollen river, she must have uttered a prayer to God to give her courage to accomplish the mission. "Be not afraid," He probably told her, and He certainly tells us still.

When we face the horrors of nature at its worst,
or the danger of life's dreaded illnesses,
or the possibility of being alone;
when the night is as black as it was in that storm for
    Kate,

when the river is as flooded,
and the possibilities of disaster as real,
we have courage, we can face danger unafraid because
He is here and with us.

The Scripture tells us how Jesus got those disciples
through another storm, and this time it was on Galilee's
lake. He will do the same for us. Our Christ with us in our
own boat is the same one who " . . . gives orders to the
winds and waves and they obey him." (Luke 8:25)

Notice God doesn't say He will spare us the chall-
enges and scary times. He does not remove life's
dangers, but He does come to see us through them carefully to the station house on the other side.

So for you whose life today brings frightening
shadows and dark, storm-filled midnights, take heart —
be filled with God's courage.

Let's take the lantern into our hands, and unafraid go
out into the night assured that God is with us.

St. Luke records Paul's farewell speech to the elders
of Ephesus like this: "But I reckon my own life to be
worth nothing to me; I only want to complete my mission
and finish the work that the Lord Jesus gave me to do
. . ." (Acts 20:24) This brings me to the second thing this
story holds out for all of us today: To have mission, to
give oneself for others, is the real satisfaction of our lives.

A poem about Kate Shelley closes like this:

Ah! Noble Kate Shelley, your mission is done;
Your deed that dark night will not fade
from our gaze,
And endless renown you have worthily won;
Let the nation be just and accord you its praise.
Let your name, let your fame
and your courage declare,
What a woman can do and a woman can dare!
(As originally reproduced by the
Heartland Educational Agency)

After Kate accomplished her feat of heroism, her life was greatly enriched because of it. All this was in addition to the fact she saved the passengers on the train and two of the four men's lives on the switch engine. It's very true that our lives are altogether different because Christ gave Himself for us on Calvary's cross. He took no thought for Himself, either. He didn't consider the salary, the discomfort, the ridicule. He had a mission to do something for us, and He did it.

Because He did it in such an unselfish way:
you and I are the saved,
we are God's children and family,
we are safe even in eternity,
we celebrate at his table of thanksgiving often.

Remember the other side is just as true. God calls us to mission, too. We have trains to warn and engineers to save. People's lives are wrecked or in danger of wrecking all around us. The storm rages nearby. Society's bridges are weak and superficial, and they often are simply a mirage.

We must go out into the night with the light of Christ and warn them as they speed along toward disaster:
Drugs and excessive drinking kill and make slaves of us.
Adultery weakens the marital bridge.
Selfishness and greed can only lead to wrecks of our lives.
Our world powers are on a course of nuclear disaster.

The powers of evil in this human existence continue to uproot, break apart, corrode away, at the very foundations of the bridges which can carry us safely across raging and troubled waters.

Let's take our mission seriously. The train is loaded with unsuspecting passengers who need to be saved from disaster. When we take God's mission seriously and go after it with enthusiasm unafraid, our lives take on good meaning and rich purpose. We move far beyond being lethargic beer drinkers and T.V. lounge lizards. Fads and "soaps" popular at the moment are of little significance.

We, too, become heroes and heroines, and a new vitality, vigor, and stimulation in life here takes hold.

There are hundreds of stories like that of fifteen-year-old Kate Shelley and the night she saved the train at Boone, Iowa. But there are none better! Nor are there any more meaningful to us on this 4th of July weekend.

Many of your fathers and mothers, some of your grand- and great-grandparents, gave themselves in the same unselfish manner, that we might be free people today. The freedom we enjoy to worship as we please, assemble when we want, and speak what we want, was very hard-won. Let us never forget or take it for granted: we travel on a track made secure for us by our ancestors.

A long railroad bridge which spans the Des Moines River up near Boone is now named the Kate Shelley High Bridge.

A drinking fountain erected in a Dubuque park was dedicated to her. The Order of Railroad Conductors gave her a gold watch and chain. At the time of her funeral, the company sent a special train to her home for the convenience of the family and hundreds of friends.

The 19th General Assembly of Iowa gave her a gold medal and $200 in cash. On the medal were these words . . . "Kate Shelley — whom neither the terror of elements, nor the fear of death could appall in her efforts to save human lives."

Today her act of heroism of over a century ago still says to us: we Christians have help in overcoming our fear. It says that to have a mission, to give oneself for others — there is the real satisfaction of life. Amen.

CHAPTER 2

The Little Brown Church
in the Wildwood

Suggested Scriptures:
Ezekiel 37:1-14
2 Corinthians 12:1-4
Luke 10:1-12, 16-20

Suggested Hymn:
"The Little Brown Church in the Wildwood"

The Little Brown Church.

We traveled to Boone County, Iowa, last week to hear of Kate Shelley, the fifteen-year-old heroine, who saved a train. We saw in her story courage and mission.

Next week we'll go to a little community south and west of Des Moines called Winterset, the birthplace of John Wayne, and learn of a farmer named Jesse Hiatt who developed the Delicious apple tree.

Today, as a part of our series of Iowa Parables, let's journey north and east of Des Moines to just a wide place in Highway 346, which used to be called Bradford and is now close to Nashua. There we discover a little frame church surrounded by oak and cedar trees along the side of the road. Only 125 families make up the present congregation, headed by Pastor John W. Christy. The church, however, is famous around the world!

Thousands have been married there [including our own Max and Alvina Cleveland]. Tourists from all over come to see the Little Brown Church — and all because of a vision set to music and now called *The Little Brown Church in the Wildwood.*

There's a church in the valley by the wildwood,
No lovelier spot in the dale;
No place is so dear to my childhood
As the little brown church in the vale. (Verse 1)

Come to the church in the wildwood,
Oh, come to the church in the vale;
No spot is so dear to my childhood
As the little brown church in the vale. (Refrain)

How sweet on a clear Sunday morning,
To list to the clear ringing bell;
Its tones so sweetly are calling,
Oh, come to the church in the vale. (Verse 3)

As you would expect, there is quite a story behind

these words made famous by the Weatherwax Brothers Male Quartet from nearby Charles City, who made the hymn their theme song and sang it at Chautauqua meetings beginning about 1910. They sang the song as part of their act and told the story of its origin, when Dr. William S. Pitts wrote its now famous words.

Oh, come to the church in the wildwood,
To the trees where the wild flowers bloom;
Where the parting hymn will be chanted,
We will weep by the side of the tomb. (Verse 2)

Hear now the famous story as Dr. Pitts told it years later.

A country school teacher of English and Scotch ancestry from Wisconsin was traveling to Fredericksburg, Iowa, in 1857, to visit his future wife. His stagecoach stopped at a prairie town of Bradford for the noon hour — they needed to take on fresh horses. Stretching his legs as he walked down Cedar Street, he was inspired by a wooded area where the church now stands. After returning to Rock County, Wisconsin, he composed the memorable song in his parents' home.

Come to the church in the wildwood,
Oh, come to the church in the vale;
No spot is so dear to my childhood
As the little brown church in the vale. (Refrain)

In 1863, when Pitts returned to Iowa to teach at Bradford Academy, he was surprised to find a little brown church in the very spot he had envisioned one six years earlier!

A Reverend John K. Nutting had led the tiny congregation, against tremendous odds, to build a frame church — and paint it with the cheapest paint possible — brown. Pastor and people had no idea a hymn had

William Pitts marker.

already been written that would make their church famous.

Pitts produced his hymn and sang it first at Bradford Academy, where he now taught. Much later, the local Weatherwax Quartet took it to practically every state in the Union and made it famous. It had described a vision which was fulfilled by God's divine providence.

The whole story of the Little Brown Church in the Wildwood is a story of vision. It is a story of permitting God to picture what is possible and daring to bring that possibility to reality.

God gives to some the privilege of vision. That's not a new phenomenon for His people.

Moses had a vision of the Promised Land atop Mount Nebo.

Paul had a vision of the Christ on the Damascus Road, and later he and Luke saw a vision of a man from Macedonia.

The disciple John had a vision of the risen Christ and of the city of Jerusalem four-square.

Spiritual leaders have had the blessing of visions in our day, too: Martin Luther had a vision of a Church free and full of grace in which every member was a priest. His namesake, Martin Luther King, Jr., had a dream of a Church free from hate and prejudice (a dream yet to be realized).

People like Zwingli, Calvin, Know, Wesley — [and Fred Weertz, who built St. Johns Church] — and modern folk like Martin Marty and Lyle Schaller and a long list of others, all have had visions. God gives to them fresh visions of how we could and ought to be. To have such a vision is a great blessing and responsibility.

The Old Testament prophet Ezekiel was given a vision of what could happen to old dry bones in a desert valley when God's very breath of life was breathed into them. He promised a preacher, if he would preach the real stuff of God's Spirit, those bones could come to life. He saw the real possibility of a new life being given to worn-out and dried up carcasses. Listen as God says, "Tell these dry bones to listen to the word of the Lord. Tell them that I, the Sovereign Lord, am saying to them: I am going to put breath into you and bring you back to life. I will give you sinews and muscles, and cover you with skin. I will put breath into you and bring you back to life. Then you will know that I am the Lord . . . Breath entered the bodies, and they came to life and stood up. There were enough of them to form an army." (Ezekiel 37:4-6, 10)

A song was written about that vision of Ezekiel, too. Our Black brothers and sisters have sung it with great glee: "Ezekiel saw them dry bones, way up in the middle of the air."

That could happen here as well. I have been given a vision, along with some others of [this congregation]. It's about *where* the Church ought to be also, and about *how* the Church ought to be. It ought to be alive and full of' spirit. Once you have the vision of how it could be, there comes a deep yearning and restlessness for change to work toward that vision's fulfillment. There comes a keen sense of expectation of God's Spirit being set free among us. Just like Pitts' vision of a church where there was no church, and just like Ezekiel's vision of life where there was no life, I have a vision of vitality and spirit and unity where those elements have been lacking.

Let's pray and look for the vision of God here in our lives and congregation.

[We have remained about the same size for years. We have quarrelled among ourselves for a long time. We have limped along with offerings less than two percent of our members' income. We have had a majority membership of spectators at our worship. Most have not studied the Bible or attended an educational opportunity since Confirmation. The presence and stimulation of the Holy Spirit have been ignored. But] we are ready — the time is right for a new vision, a vision that shows us the way and the resources and people to be the Church alive, meaningful and growing in our own day:

A Church where witnessing takes place as naturally as breathing;

Where tithing is the rule instead of the exception;

Where a vital ministry is carried out to the poor, the disenfranchized, the lonely, and they know through us God cares;

A vision of the Word of God being cherished, studied, and preached with power and conviction;

A vision of the laity taking seriously their own ministry

and mission;

One of all kinds and colors and lifestyles and sexual preferences of people coming together in God's name to worship God and love each other;

A vision of a congregation taking seriously its role as peacemakers.

Oh come, come, come, come,
Come to the church with a vision,
Oh, come to the church on Keo Way;
No spot is so precious to His mission
As the gray stone church of this day.

The blessing of vision is that it motivates, sees us through, lifts our sights and helps us see the larger picture of what could and ought to be. Then, little setbacks, discomforts, and disappointments are in proper perspective.

God's vision gives order and purpose to the future. Notice William Pitts had a vision of what could and ought to be. Not what once had been! There is always the danger of wanting to recapture the good old days, to hold everything as we think it once was, but that can never be. The Church is dynamic, it changes, it relates to the contemporary times. If, indeed, the Word became flesh and now lives among us, how that Word lives continually changes, just like how we live changes.

Especially we Lutherans, who stand in the heritage of the Reformation, the re-forming of the Church, must always have a vision for the future.

It's very dangerous to our spiritual health to look back to a certain period in our church-going — or to one preacher we liked — or to a building that was so important to us.

St. Paul wrote to his little congregation at Philippi: "The one thing I do, however, is to forget what is behind me and do my best to reach what is ahead . . ."

(Philippians 3:13)

It's nice to have sentimental attachments to little brown churches in the vale. Our day, however, calls for congregations in shopping centers, housing developments, resort areas, and where compassion to dry and poverty-stricken lands distant from Iowa might be administered.

These early Bradford settlers knew an alive Christ who had died on a cross for their sins, had beaten death and come out of a grave, and was now alive with them. The Church, then, was this "alive Christ" in their midst. It was where forgiveness is given, real presence celebrated, salvation enjoyed, concern for each other carried out, and invitation to share extended. That aliveness continues in churches in our day and time. We, too, must see God's vision and experience His liveness here in our community.

We need to find a way to educate Christian youth who play video games and watch "The Return of the Jedi," and who have their own personal computer and extreme pressure for sexual relations before the age of sixteen.

I wonder what kind of building Dr. Pitts would envision across the street from the Convention Center and just east of two massage parlors in the middle of insurance buildings and skywalks?

These are challenging times which call for visions of God's future, that Christ might be as real in our community as He was in Bradford when that congregation began. That little congregation was so blessed with a vision of what and ought to be in the days ahead, and that gave order and purpose and unity to their fellowship and ministry.

So much is possible for God's people when they share the vision. Two things made William Pitts' vision of a little brown church in the wildwood come true:

A congregation which shared the vision and worked

and was united;

Four men, called the Weatherwax Brothers Male Quartet, who dared to take that vision out into the world.

It's one thing to have a dream; it's another to get busy and make it real.

The Reverend John K. Nutting was called to the pastorate in 1859. There was no church building. They worshiped in a log house, a hotel dining room, an abandoned store with no doors or windows. The young pastor inspired the poor congregation to build a church. The pastor's salary was cut from $500 to $450 per year. Mr. and Mrs. Joseph Bird donated the land. A "bee" was organized to quarry the rock for the foundation. A man by the name of Watson gave some trees for the timber. Sanford Billings and his son-in-law, John Heald, got some men together to chop the wood. Elmore and Walter Smith, who owned the sawmill, sawed the logs. A wealthy church in Pittsfield, Massachusetts, donated $140, which was a gift from the children of a Sunday School class. The bell was given by a friend of the pastor. The building was dedicated December 29, 1864 — the vision had come true. It had come true because a congregation gave all they had, and a pastor led them forward in confidence.

It takes that kind of sharing to make visions real. Choir robes are needed and the people respond. Hungry are located and the grocery carts are filled to overflowing. Carpet and paint need to be applied and envelopes are received. Refugees are homeless and a Social Ministry Committee sponsors them. A bus is needed, a van would help, and the vision goes on!

Still after all this, at the end of 50 years, the Little Brown Church of Nashua seemed to be going the way of so many of America's rural churches. In 1910 weeds grew waist high across unkept grounds. Visitors, according to the church's history, could pull old square

nails out from of the siding. Then came that famous
Weatherwax Brothers Quartet, who took the song all
over the country, and the dry bones of Ezekiel's vision
came to life. Tom, Bill, Asa, and Les were their names;
but they might as well have been named Harold, Mary,
Jim, John, and Diane. You see, we too have an
invitation to extend, just as they did when they sang,
"Oh, come to the church in the vale."

Our church and God's vision of it can become real if
we will invite, coax, plead, and bring to the "gray stone
church in the city."

It's quite a story: William Pitts and his vision of a
church to be in a little wooded area near Nashua, Iowa. I
love how Pastor Nutting led out and held that vision
before his people and the wonderful way they
responded. I believe you and I can do that, too.

I like, also, the way those singing brothers took the
vision out into the world and how it caught on. For who
among us has not at least hummed the tune?

From the church in the valley by the wildwood,
When day fades away into night,
I would fain from this spot of my childhood
Wing my way to the mansions of light. (Verse 4)

Come to the church in the wildwood,
Oh, come to the church in the vale;
No spot is so dear to my childhood
As the little brown church in the vale. (Refrain)
Amen.

The Church in the Wildwood

W. S. P.   Dr. Wm. S. Pitts

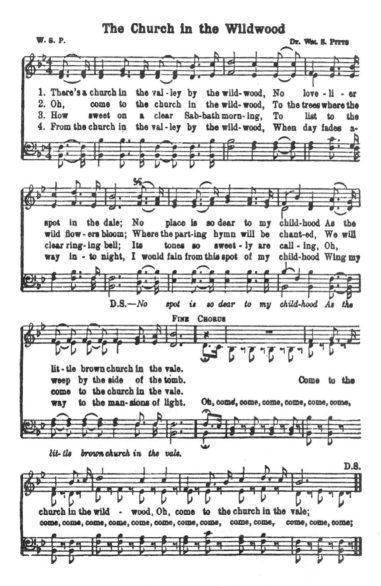

1. There's a church in the val-ley by the wild-wood, No love-li-er
2. Oh, come to the church in the wild-wood, To the trees where the
3. How sweet on a clear Sab-bath morn-ing, To list to the
4. From the church in the val-ley by the wild-wood, When day fades a-

spot in the dale; No place is so dear to my child-hood As the
wild flow-ers bloom; Where the part-ing hymn will be chant-ed, We will
clear ring-ing bell; Its tones so sweet-ly are call-ing, Oh,
way in-to night, I would fain from this spot of my child-hood Wing my

D.S.—No spot is so dear to my child-hood As the

FINE CHORUS

lit-tle brown church in the vale.
weep by the side of the tomb.
come to the church in the vale.   Come to the
way to the man-sions of light.   Oh, come, come, come, come, come, come,

lit-tle brown church in the vale.

D.S.

church in the wild-wood, Oh, come to the church in the vale;
come, come, come, come, come, come, come, come, come, come, come, come, come;

CHAPTER 3

Jesse Hiatt and His Apple Tree

Suggested Scriptures:
Genesis 3:1-7
Romans 11:13-24
Luke 13:6-9

Suggested Hymn:
"Sing to the Lord of Harvest"

Jesse Hiatt's apple tree.

In a little park in Winterset, Iowa, you can see a large boulder on which is inscribed these words:

To commemorate the discovery in Madison County, Iowa, of a variety of apple by Jesse Hiatt. A.D. 1872, and called by him the Hawkeye — sole right to propagate acquired by C. M. Stark, A.D. 1894, and by him renamed, introduced, and disseminated throughout the apple world as the Delicious apple.

The story of this Indiana Quaker gardener who moved to Madison County in the 1850s to be near his brother in East Peru is one of Iowa's most interesting parables.

Jesse Hiatt was the youngest of twelve children of a farmer and orchard grower. Jesse learned early to plant, prune, and graft trees in his father's orchard.

Married in 1845, he had five children by the mid-1850s, when he moved to take up farming on two half-sections of land not far outside Winterset. He added to the trees he brought from Indiana with a wagon load from Oskaloosa and started an orchard.

Jesse was known as a slow-moving, slow-talking Quaker and a kindly person. He had a reputation for honesty.

In 1874, Hiatt built the largest barn in Madison County. He planned next to build a house. His friends, however, talked him into building a flour mill called the Centennial. The milling went well the first couple years. Then came the chinch bug and drought and there was a drastic wheat failure.

He operated the mill at a loss for eight years. He was discouraged and worn out. He found comfort in his gardening and experimenting. He had practiced seed selection for a long time, and developed a good variety of potato and two varieties of apples called the Hiatt Black and the Hiatt Sweet.

The old man was a familiar sight in Winterset, peddling watermelons and produce from the back of his farm wagon.

Then came a discovery which would cause Jesse Hiatt's name to be inscribed on a marker in Winterset's park and remembered to this very day. In the spring of 1872, Hiatt found that a sprout from a dead Bellflower seedling had sprung a healthy shoot. He cut it off and it grew again! He decided that any tree that hardy ought to be nurtured and developed.

After a few years, the shoot, now grown into a tree, produced its first apple. When Jesse tasted it, he was certain he had the "best-tasting apple in all the world." He named the new brand "the Hawkeye apple."

The tree produced for years and Jesse sent his Hawkeye apples to Iowa fairs. His friends could see no future in this kind of tree. After eleven years of trying to promote his new Hawkeye apple, he sent some to a fruit show at Louisiana, Missouri. C. M. Stark, of Stark Brothers Nursery tasted it and knew it should be called a name he had been saving for just such special taste: "Delicious." But, Mr. Stark lost Jesse's name and address, and could not respond.

A whole year passed and Jesse heard nothing from the nursery. In 1894 persistent and patient Jesse sent more of his streaked, strawberry-colored apples with a quintet of rounded knobs to Stark Brothers. As soon as they were received, they wrote a letter and made a visit to see this tree. The propagation rights were purchased and the "Hawkeye" became the "Delicious," and eventually the favorite apple in the United States.

At the time of Hiatt's death in 1898, the Delicious apple was still unrecognized and it wasn't even mentioned in his obituary. The state horticultural society took no notice of his life's end.

A large marker was erected in the Winterset city park

in 1922 as a memorial to a patient Quaker and Iowan who gave to the world, through his persistence, the Delicious apple.

Not unlike the parables of the New Testament, this parable can tell us many things about how God is and about how we can be. First and foremost, it is a story about patience and persistence.

There is something very patient in the character of this Quaker farmer. He probably learned it from that gentle and quiet religion of his parents in Indiana.

There were numerous times when he could have given up:

the wheat failure and his mill going broke;

the usual pioneer hardships, scrimping and toiling while they broke the land;

the full year's wait after sending the apple to the Stark Company;

the county fairs when other well-known brands were honored over his.

Jesse was a patient man, as was his God — and patience is a Godly virtue that is a blessing not only to its owner, but to all those around him or her.

Jesse was like the gardener in Jesus' parable in Luke 13: " 'Cut it down! Why should it go on using up the soil?' But the gardener answered, 'Leave it alone, sir, just one more year; I will dig around it and put in some fertilizer. Then if the tree bears figs next year, so much the better; if not, then you can have it cut down.' " — Luke 13:7-9.

In the Old Testament, patience often seems to mean simply the endurance or long-suffering of present evil. Then, in Isaiah 53, we get the idea that patience has power to change that evil. However, most Old Testament references to patience describe God's quality of how *He* operates. As sinners and very imperfect and straying members of His family, we always rejoice that we have that patient, loving Father.

In the New Testament, patience moves far beyond

mere expectation of "help on the way," to a triumphant faith in the love of God. To be confident that God loves and cares for you means that you can endure a number of things and launch out in a victorious way, knowing God is with you. Paul writes to the Church of Thessalonica: "May the Lord lead you into greater understanding of God's love and the endurance that is given by Christ." — 1 Thessalonians 3:5.

The patience shown by the saints in the early Church is more than endurance of persecution without complaint: it is a lively, outgoing power of faith — an active energy, rather than a passive resignation.

St. Paul could have given up so many times. He was stoned and driven out of town, beaten, jailed, ridiculed, made fun of, shipwrecked, and framed. He had a great measure of God's endurance and patience.

We Christians have not only patient endurance to get through during difficult times; but, we have God's help in changing the circumstances and putting all that happens to us in a proper perspective.

A few years after the first Delicious trees were sent out, letters came in from all parts of the country. People were inquiring about the name of the new apple tree which tasted unlike other apples. So the Delicious apple gained national and international recognition. Mr. Stark expressed pride in such a wide distribution, but told people that this came about at great expense and patience.

We Christians have an active energy in our faith, rather than a passive resignation. That's the way God's people ought to be. Just like Jesse Hiatt, patiently cultivating and promoting his apple tree, who could have become a bitter old man because he never got the recognition coming him. He could have become bitter because God gave him a "dirty deal" by bringing drought and the chinch bugs. He could have gone inside that new home of his, closed the curtains, and cursed all those who "have it good." But he didn't! He had God's patience, and patience and perseverence is what his life story is all about.

Today there are thousands of Delicious apple trees all around the world in orchards and thousands more in our back yards.

This summer's Stark Brothers spring catalog advertised the Delicious apple tree this way:

> *Red Delicious Apple. The world's most popular red apple. Stark Brothers paid $25,000 for the original tree . . . It gets its exceptional quality and flavor from the parent tree, the world-famous Stark Delicious.*

Let's learn from this Iowa parable:

> *We may not be able to answer why.*
> *It may seem we're making no progress.*
> *Someone else may have disappointed us.*
> *It may seem like the job should be available now.*
> *We may want to ask why God takes so long to answer.*
> *Someone is so agonizingly slow to act and we are so anxious.*

But God is still here, and He is in charge yet. We do have His family and spirit to get us through. So when our loved ones do the same dumb things over and over, and when we make the same foolish mistakes again and again, and when we try and try and seem to get nowhere, Jesse shows us patience. It is the same resilient, gentle, trusting patience that carried him through drought, silence, and lack of respect, and that caused the erection of a marker in the Winterset park in memory of him and his apples.

This is also a parable about small beginnings. That

Bellflower sprout came up from a dead stump and was cut off like a weed, but it persisted! From one sprout came millions of apple trees all over the world.

I have traveled to East Peru to see the famous apple tree. The original was killed by the Armistice Day freeze in 1940. The Stark Company lease on the tree had expired in January of 1934. A. W. B. Landis, who then owned the land, gave the tree excellent care until it died. But surprise upon surprise, from its roots have sprung two sizeable trees with the same luscious apples as the original. Around the collapsed house, weeds of the barnyard, and general run-down condition of the living part of the farm, are a number of Delicious apple trees that have replaced the old and original one. It's now on the Tracey property. A couple sprouts from the original tree grow on either side of the marker in the park at Winterset.

It's a serendipity story, isn't it? It's just full of surprises! That's the way it is in God's Kingdom, too. Jesus taught us: From seeds planted in the most unlikely soil, from a tiny mustard seed comes that flowering tree, and He goes on to put a lot of significance on the small and what we are accustomed to calling unimportant. A lily, a pinch of salt, a sparrow falling from the heavens, a beat-up man in the side ditch, a crazy little person up a tree, a woman of the street in Bethany: He teaches us that in His Kingdom, the little is loaded with possibilities.

Like that brand of apples, it all begins small; we trust, God nurtures and blesses, and great things are the result.

St. Paul tells us in today's lesson that we Gentiles are like a wild olive tree branch grafted into a cultivated olive tree. We often get it reversed and think of ourselves as the bigshots and the pure Christians. Not so, says Paul! "You Gentiles are like the branch of a wild olive tree that is broken off and then, contrary to nature, is joined to a cultivated alive tree . . ." — Romans 11:24.

We shouldn't be swelled up with pride, but rejoicing

with amazement that God takes us on, we who are so unpromising and imperfect.

Jesus went into His ministry around Galilee showing what was possible in what the people thought was impossible. He begins small with a birth to an unwed teenage mother in a cow barn; He continues with childhood in a backwater town; a ministry with only 12 followers who were oddballs of society; crucifixion as a common criminal; and burial in a borrowed tomb.

Who, living next door to the kid growing up in Nazareth would have dreamed what that Galilean carpenter could accomplish? Victory over death, life beyond the grave, and back to live with us now in Spirit, convincing and empowering us to love one another — that's what He accomplished.

Today a thousand people come to this place called the Church, a place dedicated to Him, thriving halfway around the world from where it began so small so long ago.

And during His ministry He pointed out those great possibilities where we just don't see them:

in a prostitute at a well,

in an abrasive blind beggar along Jericho's road,

in a fisherman who was crude and rambunctious,

in some children brought to Him for a blessing though the disciples thought them a bother,

in a widow who gave her mite in the temple offering,

and in some loaves and a couple fish.

That's the way it's been for God's people down through the years. The world complains and says, "Why me?" We persist and trust and know victory. The world surveys and analyzes and says, "It can't be done!" We pray for His help and finish the task. The world says, "It's not important," and we point out "Such is the Kingdom of God."

If I had time, I'd develop a completely different emphasis in this parable's lessons. It would have to do with those things we do now which will never benefit us, but which will mean a great deal to people and God's world in the future. Jesse sold the rights to his apple tree and thus could build a new house for his wife Rebecca and himself, right beside the now-famous tree. But he never knew of the fame of his Delicious apples. His house now lays in ruin, fallen down in a heap among the weeds of the farm's barnyard. Wild sprouts of Delicious apple trees abound. But, think how many have enjoyed his apples, and still do, all over the world.

He was patient and saw the possibilities, and he was willing to give so that future generations would have it better. Planting a tree, conserving resources and land, building a church, working for peace, putting your church in your will, providing scholarships — these, too, are the things of God for the days ahead.

Jesse Hiatt, 1826-1898

The monument in Winterset's park is a terrific memorial to a man named Jesse Hiatt — a gentle Quaker man who saw the possible in what the world called insignificant. Above all he demonstrated for us the great Christian virtues of persistence and patience.

Frank Fenemous, a California veteran fruit grower, wrote in 1912, having grown Delicious apples a few years: "Jesse Hiatt, in growing that original tree of Delicious, reared to himself a shiny monument that is fast spreading its branches over the apple-loving world . . . Its fruit will be a joy and satisfaction to generations unborn. No earthly hero of war and conquest ever bequeathed such rich inheritance to the world." — Page 21 of "The Delicious Apple, 100 years — 1872-1972," by Henry C. Miller.

While the apple is indeed delicious, the lesson is even more tasty. We see in the impossible and insignificant great importance and possibility; and, good friend, persistence and patience is God's great gift. Amen.

CHAPTER 4

The Plough in the Oak Tree

Suggested Scriptures:
Psalm 55
1 Peter 1:3-9
Luke 6:43-45 or Luke 9:51-62

Suggested Hymn:
"O God, Our Help in Ages Past"

Author Schmalenberger with plough in tree.

Last week from our series of Iowa Parables we heard of a peculiar man who moved to a farm outside Winterset, Iowa, and developed the now-famous Delicious apple tree. His name was Jesse Hiatt. He taught us patience and possibility.

Next week our parable comes from a true story at Belle Plaine, when they tried to dig a well and hit such a gusher they couldn't get it stopped for over a year! It's a parable of grace.

Jesus, the Christ, often told a story to lay alongside a great religious truth, or, sometimes pointed to something unusual nearby to illustrate what He was trying to teach about God.

Who doesn't remember the lilies of the field, the sower of the seed, the lost sheep, or the good shepherd?

Today's Iowa Parable is about a plough in an oak tree.

Luke or Matthew might have told it like this: "And they were going up to Des Moines from Omaha, when they stopped halfway in Danish country to rest and eat. Traveling a short distance up Route 71, they came to a shaded roadside park near the village of Exira, and there decided they would eat their picnic. And behold, as the meal was being laid out, some of them wandered about the park and came upon an ancient oak tree, which had embedded in it a single-bottom farm plough. 'Master,' they said, 'How strange is this that a plough should be completely embedded in a beautiful oak tree. Tell us the meaning of this thing we have found at an Iowa roadside park.' He sat them down and told them the story of the Plough in the Oak Tree, as recorded by the Historical Society and handed down from one generation of Iowans to another."

Some have said that a farmer by the name of Andrew Jackson Leffingwell of Exira leaned that plough against the little oak sapling after becoming discouraged with trying to farm the Audubon County land. He left the farm never to return, to take up mercantile business. That's almost right!

Mrs. Anna Foss, who lives nearby, has told me how the whole episode really took place. Mrs. Foss' uncle, Christian Miller, was a Danish immigrant and hired hand on the Andrew Leffingwell farm. For three days he tried to make the single-bottom ploughshare scour as it should. So it was leaned against the little scrub of an oak tree in a grove on a grassy knoll near the railroad track.

Christian Miller enlisted in the military at Fort Omaha. Years later, after Chris had married, he and his son, Andrew Miller, were driving past the Leffingwell farm, and he remembered the plough.

The plough was exposed to the public in the late '20s, when U.S. Highway 71 was developed. The tree and plough had become one!

Chris Miller died in 1932. Andrew J. Leffingwell's granddaughter married John Miller and remembers clearly her uncle's story about the plough in the tree. A nephew of Chris Miller still lives in Exira and confirms this account.

Over 1,000 tourists a year from 34 states have registered at the little park named the Plough in the Oak Tree Park. Many local families, in addition, use the park, which is now leased from Wilmer Peterson, a Harlan banker, by the Exira Garden Club.

All this because Christian Miller, a hired hand for Andrew Leffingwell, farmer, gave up on a plough and parked it in discouragement and decided to enlist in the Army.

"After He finished the story, the little band of disciples was amazed and asked what meaning this could have for them. He explained that He spoke in parables so they could understand God's great truths, and that many would pass by and never see, and others would see but not understand. Then He opened His mouth and said these words: 'Verily, verily, I say unto you: That which seems like defeat, God can turn into our great opportunities.' "

Andrew Leffingwell and Christian Miller had just plain become discouraged. The land was dry and contrary, the plough wouldn't scour correctly, the weather was terrible and the market no better; it just all seemed hopeless. So they gave up. Probably with some choice Danish words, Chris Miller plopped that old plough, which he had dragged through so much Iowa sod, against a tiny unpromising oak tree sprout, and departed for the Army.

But God didn't give up! Because now there are beautiful fields of corn, beans, and wheat growing on that same land. In addition, that little sprout of an oak tree quietly, but consistently, grew and grew and grew. Around the sharp plough bottom, around the handle, engulfing the single-tree neck, nurtured by the good earth, the rain and sunshine, it grew, until a reminder of despair and discouragement had become a great monument to God's progress, His purpose, and even when it all seems hopeless to us.

That's the way it is in God's Kingdom. Oh, there are setbacks. There are difficult times when you wonder, "Where in the world is God and why doesn't He help?" It can appear as though God is saying by His seeming lack of concern: "Give up — It's just not worth the effort." But just as that oak tree continues quietly and, almost unnoticed, to grow and progress, so does His Kingdom in our world and day.

Today's Iowa Parable is about discouragement and a remedy for it.

So if the kids have severly disappointed you,
if your job seems impossible,
if you've gotten nowhere in your witnessing to
the faith,
if you're getting older without accomplishing
what you wanted to,

*if the continual hassle for enough money to make
    ends meet get worse instead of better,
or if you just can't seem to get well,*

this story about Christian Miller and Andy Leffingwell of
Exira, Iowa, is especially for you.

To be discouraged, like Chris and Andy, is not new
or unique to us in our age. The Psalmist knew the feeling.

Psalm 55

*Hear my prayer, O God;
    don't turn away from my plea!
Listen to me and answer me;
    I am worn out by my worries
I am terrified by the threats of my enemies,
    crushed by the oppression of the wicked.
I am terrified,
    and the terrors of death crush me.
I see violence and riots in the city,
    surrounding it day and night,
    filling it with crime and trouble.
There is destruction everywhere;
    the streets are full of
    oppression and fraud.
But I call to the Lord God for help
    and he will save me.
Morning, noon, and night
    my complaints and groans go up to him,
    and he will hear my voice.
Leave your troubles with the Lord
    and he will defend you
    he never lets honest people be defeated.*

It may seem the powers that work against God are
winning, and perhaps for a while they are, but you and I
know the ultimate victory is ours.

Often, the most severe setbacks are opportunites for growth in our Christian faith. Jesus promised, "Blessed are those who mourn . . . Blessed are those who are persecuted for my sake."

While God doesn't cause these disappointments to come upon us, He loves us so much that He gives us the opportunity to turn them around and make them opportunities for blessings.

Someone we love dies, and we learn of close friends we didn't know we had.

A spouse has a close brush with illness and death, and we discover just what love we have for each other, and a new and deeper relationship develops.

We lose our job and learn about Christian concern and caring.

We don't achieve our goal in life and discover it wasn't one that held real significance anyway.

And Christian Miller of Exira gives up and throws his plough down on a tender oak shoot and a park is created where hundreds each year can gather on the grass and enjoy the shade of that now-enormous tree.

So God takes the "no" of this discouraged farmer and hired hand, and turns it into an "Iowa Parable," with promise and hope from the pulpit of this church today.

See how the most severe setbacks can be turned around as great blessings? It's when we let God be with us and in them. The writer of Psalm 55 ends by saying, "As for me, I will trust in you." (vs. 23)

God does not cause us adversity in order to bless us. He does, however, take whatever trouble this imperfect life brings, and gives us a way, with His help, to turn it around for a great blessing.

St. Paul wrote to the Christians who were discouraged in Rome: "We know that in all things God works for good with those who love him . . ." (Romans

8:28) Luke tells how Jesus promised in His parable about a tree and its fruit: "A good person brings good out of the treasure of good things in his heart . . ." (Luke 6:45) So, when our roots are deep in God's spiritual life, we can handle whatever comes our way and even cause good to come out of it.

There's a large oak tree in a little park near Exira, Iowa. If it could talk, it would tell you of the pain of having that sharp plough laid upon it. Yet, it grew with its painful situation and made a happy contribution to its world. Those who sit in its shade and marvel at the extraordinary tree know God's promise — He will turn our defeats into blessings.

In the Christian faith, death is turned into life. There was a certain Friday in Jerusalem when it seemed that all that was good and right and God-like had been killed. It appeared that discouragement had won out forever. No doubt those disciples had fled in fear, embarrassment, and discouragement, to gather again in the upper room and "lick their wounds." Some felt all was lost. It had been an exciting three years, but they had been defeated.

People who hated and were full of what is ugly and wrong had beat them and put their Lord on Calvary's cross. Maybe Joseph of Arimathea could get by with putting all their hopes in his rock tomb and sealing away God's attempt to come and be with them. Then came glorious Easter, and it became clear that those hopes and dreams, all their efforts and sacrifices, had not been in vain, for God had breathed growth and life and hope into what seemed so hopeless. The dead Christ out of the grave and alive, they could regroup; there was new vision; bravery was given where only fear had been felt. That's the way it is to be one of God's people. Even when all seems hopeless, God gives promise and new hope. Where it seems as though there is no chance at all, God gives a resurrection, new life, and often even better life.

There are countless examples of death and new life in

our own experience:

The last child leaves home, and for the first time the nest is empty. (We rediscover our wife or husband.)

The divorce is final, and we find ourselves without a spouse. (New and more sensitive friendships develop in the Christian community.)

Our boyfriend or girlfriend sends the "Dear John" letter. (We gain maturity and a more compatible partner turns up.)

Our business investments go sour and we lose our money. (And we learn possessions don't have to be present to have a deep and meaningful life.)

Our kids bitterly disappoint us. (And we discover we can't merely live for our children, and we develop our own personality and satisfaction.)

Sometimes we go through the Good Friday experience in our own lives. All we hope for is shattered and taken from us. Sometimes it seems as though Easter will never come again. But it does! The tree continues to grow!

Oftentimes we are tempted to give up and despair just short of God's resounding and glad-filled resurrection — glorious Easter. If we'll just persist, hang on and hang in there, an Easter, a resurrection, a blessing, is on the way for us, too.

If we'll look carefully and pray fervently, God will, indeed, help us to not only get through and experience a new life, but also to grow, to learn, and to mature. We can even develop a richer and more blessed life from now on.

In his Epistle of hope, Peter wrote to us: "Because of his great mercy he gave us new life by raising Jesus Christ from death. This fills us with a living hope, and so we look forward to possessing the rich blessings that God keeps for his people. Be glad about this, even though it may now be necessary for you to be sad for a while because of the many kinds of trials you suffer. Then you will receive praise and glory and honor on the Day when Jesus Christ is revealed." (1 Peter 1:3, 4, 6, 7b)

If you travel to Danish country in Audubon County just outside Exira, you can see embedded in a large oak tree Andrew Jackson Leffingwell's plough, which would not scour correctly for Christian Miller, his hired hand. It's a pleasant little place on the edge of the Wilmer Petersen farm. Take a good look at that tree and the plough protruding from each side of its large trunk. It's an Iowa Parable. It says to us:

In the Christian faith, death is turned into life.
Often the most severe setbacks are opportunities
for growth.
That which seems like defeat, God can turn into
our great opportunities.

Next week, Belle Plaine's Gusher. Amen.

CHAPTER 5

Belle Plaine's Gusher

Suggested Scriptures:
Deuteronomy 7:7-11
Ephesians 2:4-10
Luke 11:1-13

Suggested Hymn:
"Come, Thou Fount of Every Blessing

8th Street and 8th Avenue, Belle Plaine.

Last week we traveled west over Interstate 80 to Exira, Iowa, to hear about Andrew Leffingwell's plough stuck in an oak tree. We found there a parable of new life and hope for our discouraging times.

This Sunday we'll travel east on Interstate 80, and again get off and go a little to the north to Belle Plaine. On the south side of town, we'll see a boulder with a bronze plaque which marks the spot of what newspaper people back in 1886 called "The Eighth Wonder of the World." It's one of Iowa's parables about God's grace.

St. Paul taught us, "It is by God's grace that you have been saved . . . He did this to demonstrate for all time to come the extraordinary greatness of his grace in the love he showed us in Christ Jesus." (Ephesians 2:5b, 7)

We have learned that God's amazing grace is something that flows to us undeserved, it certainly can be misused, and it often remains untapped.

So back to Jumbo, Belle Plaine's gusher, to illustrate just how great God's grace is. It all started when the village of Belle Plaine hired William Wier for $350 to dig a well for the city and the south side's schoolhouse. On August 26, 1886, at 1:30 p.m., the well-digger struck water at 193 feet. The next day he returned to find a large amount of water belching into the air. The well increased in size all that day. The flow enlarged to one-and-a-half feet wide, spurting eight feet into the air! William Wier quietly left town.

The water spout, dubbed "Jumbo," got larger and larger. The citizens of the little town were excited, then frantic, and almost crazy. The two-inch hole was now expanded to three feet in diameter, as rocks and sand roared from its gaping mouth. The City Council couldn't get Jumbo shut off. Months went by, and two streams over twelve feet wide developed to carry the water to the Iowa River.

Of course, the press traveled to Belle Plaine from all over and terribly exaggerated the well's size and effect.

Sketches were drawn and published of rescuing Belle Plaine's citizens from second-floor windows! It was described in distant newspapers as "water spouting hundreds of feet into the air with a roar that could be heard from miles around."[1]

Soon people claimed magical cures performed by drinking its water. They tried a lot of different ways to stop the tremendous flow of water, but to no avail. A man from Marshalltown by the name of Luther King was hired for $2,000 to cap the now-famous artesian gusher. He started to build a high wooden fence around it, and charged spectators to get in and see the strange fountain of Belle Plaine. Finally, as a last resort, the Council engaged the services of a local foundry, Palmer Brothers. On October 16, 1887, thirteen months after the well was opened, it was closed with hydraulic jacks and great quantities of sand and cement. An asphalt road now covers the place where Jumbo gushed forth.

Before they got the geyser quieted down, there had been dumped into its gaping mouth 200 feet of pipe, 40 carloads of stone, and 130 barrels of cement.

It's an unusual story of a well that went berserk and showed a whole community the latent power of water that lay just 200 feet below its surface. I call it the "Parable of Belle Plaine's Gusher." It's one of Iowa's greatest.

I'm rather sure that William Wier, contractor King from Marshalltown, and the City Council, would not agree, but God's grace is like this artesian well of Belle Plaine — free and plentiful!

His grace comes without effort on our part — it's God's gift and usually a surprise. Grace means "gift" — it is central to our Christian belief:

that God's love for us,

his saving action,

---

1. *Tell a Tale of Iowa* by Don Brown; Wallace-Homestead Book Company, Des Moines, Iowa.

his help in our suffering and trouble, is all a gift.
It just pours out to us like "Jumbo" of Belle Plaine.
St. Paul writes, "All who receive God's *abundant* grace
and are freely put right with him will rule in life through
Christ." Romans 5:17b.

When we kneel for Communion, when we are
adopted by Baptism, that life-giving and death-protecting
gift of grace was, and is, God's gift to us. It is not
deserved; it is not earned or even expected. Dr. Joseph
Sittler, Lutheran theologian, said of infant baptism: "It's a
recognition that we weren't consulted in the first place."

It's no accident we use water when we baptize with
God's grace. We even call the baptismal container a
"font." "Font" comes from "fountain" and, much like
Belle Plaine's gusher, from this well of grace God comes
with His many blessings.

God's grace doesn't run out, either! Scripture assures
us God's love and grace is all-sufficient. It doesn't run
out, wear out, or dribble away for lack of supply. The
hymn, "There's a Wideness in God's Mercy," assures us,
"There is grace enough for thousands . . ."

We may have come to God's grace-well many times
before, but we are always welcome to return for more.
There is no rationing; you don't have to have shirt and
shoes to get it, either. We may have resolved, the last
time we received His grace, we would do better and be
better, and here we are again at His table and before His
altar. God loves; He's still here with His gift of
forgiveness. We may have gone into the far country
many times, but our Heavenly Father still rushes down
the road to greet us and welcome us home and back into
the family.

Jesus tells a parable to illustrate this idea. He told of
men who worked just one hour of the day and got paid
the same as those who worked all day long.

It surprises us when and where we least expect it. Old
William Wier got a surprise when he returned the next

day. Boy, did he have a well! God surprises us, too —
His grace spurts forth at some of the most peculiar times:

when someone dies,
at the birth of a child,
during the singing of a hymn,
when we grow bitter at someone else,
at the hospital bed,
when we have strayed and guilt burns in our bellies,
in visiting a neighbor,
in loving a spouse,
in the loneliness of the late night,
before the humdrum and routine meal.
God gives grace, and we are blessed and surprised.

And like the gusher of Belle Plaine, grace is available
to everyone. No one can build a fence around it, even
though they try. Like a fresh and lovely lagoon in a public
park, all can gather around and be cooled, comforted,
washed, and inspired. Like a public drinking fountain in
the center of town, all can come and have their thirst
quenched. There are no restrictions, no requirements, no
superficial barriers. Race, sex, education status, color,
nationality — these make no difference. God's grace is
for all.

Old Jumbo, August 28, 1886

The more we receive, the more there is available to us. That's right — like "Jumbo" that got larger and larger, once we accept and receive God's gift of amazing grace, it just opens up to us more and more.

Listen to the parable Jesus tells in Luke 11: " . . . Ask, and you will receive; seek, and you will find; knock, and the door will be opened to you. For everyone who asks will receive, and he who seeks will find, and the door will be opened to anyone who knocks." (Luke 11:9-10)

This grace never stops expanding and flowing. We are a lot like William Wier each day we return to our God.

The water in the Belle Plaine gusher was tested by the Chicago and Northwestern Railroad Company. It was found to be unsuitable for use in locomotives, and word was spread not to drink it. Nevertheless, people did, and before long the word was out it could heal. One man had been given only a few weeks to live, but claimed after he drank the water, he was completely healed. A Mr. J. Baker wrote, "For 30 years I have suffered with dyspepsia and its comitant troubles, and suffered much from nervous exhaustion. The use of the Belle Plaine Mineral Water has greatly benefited me. Have not been so well in ten years."

God's grace — His well — is healing, too. In fact, we describe health and "being all right" with the word "well." Come to this well where you are given a gift of love and forgiveness and healing can take place. Not only for troubled and distraught minds, but for difficulty in the marriage, strife with the parents and kids, and other human relationships which are tearing you apart. When we let God's grace work in our own lives, healing can take place where we have hurt each other. And healing, too, can happen when our physical being has disintegrated because of worry, stress, guilt, and lack of self-worth.

You and I can sing with the choir today those same words:

I've got peace like a river,
joy like a fountain,
faith like the ocean.

God's grace is, indeed, like Belle Plaine's gusher, because it just pours out without our deserving, and all we need do is gather around and marvel at it.

As wonderful as this grace of God can be, there are those who would misuse it. Like Luther King who came from Marshalltown, who had a man go down into the well in a diving suit several times and built a fence around it in order to sell admissions, our use of God's free and abundant grace can be terribly commercial. Some would reduce the business of the Church to a commercial venture. All discussions can be made on the basis of profit and loss, rather than God's mission. We have a great well gushing forth, and our main job is to get that grace out to all who have need of it.

It is for this reason I have serious doubts about the legitimacy of some TV preachers like Oral Roberts, Pat Robertson, and Jerry Falwell. To me they look like a Mr. King, who built that fence and charged to get in.

Sometimes it's too easy to take credit for what God gives. Old welldriller Wier got quite a surprise the next morning. John Newton, in his hymn "Amazing Grace," writes:

Twas grace that taught my heart to fear,
And grace my fears relieved;
How precious did that grace appear,
The hour I first believed. (Verse 2)

To take credit for our grand Church or ministry — for God's great blessings here — would be as silly as William Wier standing by the gusher, flexing his suspenders and bragging, "Look what I did!"

I think most of us are more like the driller when he

quietly got out of town the next morning. That was more well than he wanted to take responsibility for! We behave in a similar fashion. We have an infant baptized and never come to worship again. We are confirmed on Pentecost and leave the fellowship of believers until marriage. We make all those religious vows before God's altar and then tell the spouse to do the church work. It's tempting to be like that frightened welldriller and quietly leave town!

It reminds me of the church member who is ill in the hospital, expects the pastor to find him on his own, and be right there. He is prayed for and visited, comforted and given private communion, and is healed. He returns home, calls himself lucky, and refuses to pledge at the next stewardship drive.

After all, Christian stewardship is figuring out, as we stand by God's abundant grace-well, how to respond properly to the flood of blessings God pours out on us. It is then to share this abundant gift with others who need it. So often we just bathe in all this resource for the good life, drinking and cooling ourselves, and then walk away with William Wier, taking no responsibility for all that we have received.

Paul writes, " . . . God's grace is much greater, and so is his free gift to so many people through the grace of one man, Jesus Christ." (Romans 5:15)

Let's remember Wier and King and how easy it is to misuse this wonderful grace.

God's grace remains untapped for most of us. If you go to the corner of 8th Avenue and 8th Street next to Charlie Stall's place in Belle Plaine today, there is only a paved street over all that hydraulic power and a piece of granite with a bronze plaque along the curb that marks the location of the phenomenon. It was placed there on December 3, 1954, by the Ladies of Artesia Chapter of the Daughters of the American Revolution. For a number of years, townspeople walked around the place, keeping their eyes on the spot, a little uneasy that it might erupt and gush forth again.

We tip-toe around our church in similar fashion — this place where there is so much grace power and where the well is abundant and plentiful.

If we ever set free all this which God would like to pour out into our congregation and into our community, what drastic changes could take place. Even more than an artesian well gone berserk, our witnessing to the forgiveness available and the love of one another and for enemies, could baptize this congregation and community in a new spirit.

I think of that when I step to the baptismal font, of how much it is like the gusher of Belle Plaine. Can't you see the pastor dipping his hand down into the container, and somehow setting all that power loose in our midst? The water would be spouting to the ceiling. [Harold Parry,] our Property Manager, would be calling the Property Committee together to decide what to do. [Marve Behrens,] our maintenance man, would be running for a mop. [Butch Lorentzen or Walt Schlievert,] plumbers, would be going for their pipe wrenches. And the Altar Guild would try their best to keep the Paschal Candle burning.

This baptismal water has that kind of power. But we often treat it so casually and drop a little moisture on the head of a child in a pious fashion. There is power in that font and grace in that water. Our worship service ought to be like dancing and playing in and around that water, much like children do in and through a lawn sprinkler on a hot day in Iowa.

In January of 1957, on the Elmer Jones farm southeast of Belle Plaine, a well was drilled. After it was capped, water worked its way outside of the casing and the cap had to be removed. Six tons of crushed rock were used to stop the flow. Three weeks later, the well broke loose again. The pressure lost caused other wells in the area to slow or cease. The well was finally recased and ceased being troublesome. At the writing of this sermon, no other "gushers" have broken loose, but the possibility is ever present around Belle Plaine. There is power just below the surface there . . . and it's here, too.

The cross of Jesus Christ is a lot like Belle Plaine's "Jumbo." In it is power and it gives to us unexpected and undeserved water of life:

a chance to start over,
a sense of self-worth,
life after this earthly one,
a way to love the unlovely,
His Spirit with us here,
a new and good relationship with our God.

What a story — a well that just couldn't be stopped! It's an Iowa parable about how God gives to us in a surprising and so very generous way. It tells us:

For so many, God's grace remains untapped.
God's grace can be terribly misused.
His grace is like an artesian well — free and
    plenty. It comes to us on its own.

"It is by God's grace that you have been saved . . . He did this to demonstrate for all time to come the extraordinary greatness of his grace . . ." (Ephesians 2:5b, 7) Amen.

CHAPTER 6

The Bloomer Girl
From Council Bluffs

Suggested Scriptures:
Judges 4:4-10, 14-16
Galatians 3:23-29
Luke 18:1-8

Suggested Hymn:
"Rise Up, O Saints of God!"

In these last weeks we've looked at some of the places, events, and people who make up Iowa's heritage. I've called them "Iowa Parables," and from them have tried to illustrate great Christian truths. Today we'll look at "The Bloomer Girl from Council Bluffs."

In perusing the history of our great state, two things strike me as very obvious. First, the white people are always the winners. I've noticed that when Indians kill white settlers, it is called a massacre. When white people kill Indians, it's called a victory.

The second thing is not quite as obvious: men get all the credit for Iowa progress. History, art, and media were, and still are, male-dominated. Yet, in selecting the Iowa greats — those "doers" and "shakers" who have left their impact and made a difference for us all — I would select four women right at the top of the list:

1. Jessie Field Shambaugh, who was born in Shenandoah, Iowa, in 1882, who became the Superintendent of Schools in Page County. Often called the "First Lady of the Cornfields," Jessie founded the 4-H Clubs of America. She was a great friend of youth and their education.
2. Arabella Babb Mansfield from Des Moines County, born in 1846, who became the first woman admitted to the Bar of both the State of Iowa and the United States. It was in June of 1869. Arabella was also the founder of the "Iowa Woman's Suffrage Association."
3. Carrie Chapman Catt, first woman Superintendent of

Amelia Bloomer.

Schools in Mason City, a teacher, feminist, and lecturer. She was President of the national Woman Suffrage Association and held that position when the 19th Amendment to the Constitution, giving women the right to vote, was passed. In 1919 she founded the National League of Women Voters, and in 1925 she began crusading against war and founded the National Committee on Cause and Cure of War. I sure would have liked to have known her.

These are, indeed, great leaders of our state and nation from Iowa. But, one other intrigues me the most. She is, indeed, one of Iowa's most interesting parables. By now, Sally Ride has flown in the space shuttle and Sandra Day O'Connor has written her first major Supreme Court dissent. But let's go back in time, better than 150 years ago, and learn of Amelia Jenks Bloomer. She was a woman who would have been comfortable in the company of such as Sally Ride, Sandra Day O'Connor, and Gloria Steinem.

Amelia Jenks was born in New York in 1818, began teaching at the age of seventeen, and married Dexter Bloomer, a newspaper editor, in 1840. At their wedding 143 years ago, she persuaded the minister to omit the word "obey" from the marriage vows!

Amelia and Dexter moved to Mount Vernon, Ohio, where she published a journal called *The Lily*. In it she crusaded against drinking and the subserviance of women to men in our society.

From Dexter's journal we learn that Amelia hired a woman typesetter to work on her paper, and the other male workers promptly declared they would not work with a woman. So Amelia fired them all and hired women to replace them. She was a woman who practiced what she preached.

The Bloomers moved to Council Bluffs, Iowa, in 1855. Amelia shocked the entire country by suggesting that women should rebel against the domination of men in the matter of clothing. To demonstrate her own attitude, Amelia wore a short dress, not quite to the knees, and full pantalets gathered in ruffles at her shoetops.

The new dress for women swept the country and Europe and was named "bloomers," after Amelia.

Once, when a Reverend Dr. Talmage gave a sermon in which he quoted Moses as authority for women not wearing men's attire, Amelia wrote as follows: "There are laws of fashion and dress older than Moses . . . The first fashion we have any record of was set for us by Adam and Eve, and we are not told that there was any difference in the styles worn by them." "And they sewed fig leaves together and made themselves aprons." (Genesis 3:7) "Nothing there," wrote Amelia, "to indicate that his apron was bifurcated, and hers not; that hers were long, and his short. We are led to suppose that they were just alike."

"In Genesis 3:21, God made them 'coats of skins and clothed them.' No command to her that she must swathe and cripple herself in long, tight, heavy, dragging skirts, while he dons the more comfortable, healthy garment. Common sense teaches us that the dress which is the most convenient, and the best adapted to our needs, is the proper dress for both men and women to wear." *Life and Writings of Amelia Bloomer*, page 76.

In 1855, when Amelia Jenks Bloomer and her husband came to Council Bluffs, it was a scandal. Such radicals! Yet, within 14 years, Dexter was elected mayor of the city. The Bloomers became one of the most prominent families in Western Iowa. Amelia did not remain silent, living in the shadow of her husband's skills and profession. She traveled the country, lecturing to groups and speaking for the cause of the right for women to vote.

She was known as a quiet and charming person.

In 1856, she caused the Nebraska Legislature to consider granting women suffrage. During the Civil War she organized the *Soliders Aid Society*. And in 1869, Amelia Jenks Bloomer was a founder of the Iowa Woman Suffrage Association.

That same year, Amelia became a good friend of Des Moines' Annie Savery, who became secretary of the Suffrage Society. They collaborated and cooperated and worked together on the cause of women's rights for the remainder of their lives.

Meanwhile, an admirer on the staff of *The Carpet-Bag* waxed poetically:

> *The maids were very beautiful*
> *with ebon locks and tresses,*
> *But what so much enhanced their charms*
> *were those short Bloomer dresses.*

So here's another great Iowan and a person who made a difference in how it is for Iowans and humans, both male and female, around the world. She's the "Bloomer Woman from Council Bluffs." Let's look at her cause and see today if it is also our cause, we who are called Christians and God's people.

We simply have to admit that the Bible is sexist in its reporting and its language. It reflects the attitudes of its day. All of the Bible, except perhaps Hebrews, was written by men from a male point of view. In reporting the events of the life of Christ, and certainly in the early Church, women just don't get the credit or space they deserve.

Great female spiritual heroines are given little space in the scriptures.

Mary, the mother of our Lord;
Mary Magdalene, one of Christ's disciples;
Lydia, leader of the early Church;
Sarah, the Mother of the Hebrew race;

Deborah, a leader into the Promised Land;

Mary and Martha of Bethany, Jesus' closest friends;

Priscilla, the earliest Christian missionary and businesswoman.

Yet it is true, the early Church was full of slaves and women. Out in the world they were treated less well than animals. But in the Church, these who were the outcasts of society were for the first time in their lives treated as humans and important to God.

St. Paul writes very good theology about no barriers, but his prejudices against women are blatant from time to time. It could be true that he had a Jewish wife because he had been a rabbi, and that this Jewish wife refused to convert to the Christian faith. If that's true, it may have given him a very difficult and prejudiced point of view toward females.

Consequently, we must be very careful in our quoting of Scripture as we look at what is right and God-like for our Christian family. We must always be mindful of *when* and *to whom* Scripture was written, always in the light of its context, and the spirit of the entire Bible.

Amelia wrote, "The present legal distinctions between the sexes have been made by men and not by God. Man has degraded woman from her high position in which she was placed as his companion and equal, and made of her a slave to be bought and sold at his pleasure. He has brought the Bible to prove that he is her lord and master, and taught her that resistance to his authority is to resist God's will. I deny that the Bible teaches any such doctrine. God made them different in sex, but equal in intellect, and gave them equal dominion." *Life and Writing of Amelia Bloomer*, page 62.

The Christian Church of our day does not always champion what it ought to either! Some denominations and preachers, in the name of God, are still promoting blatant sexism. Our own Lutheran Church has ordained women only in the last decade, and most positions of leadership are still male-dominated. It is only in the last four years that we have cleaned up the language of our hymnody and our liturgy to make it all-inclusive. And we still have a way to go with a lot of the materials published by our Church so that they reflect the inclusiveness which is ours in the Body of Christ.

Most congregations have blindly followed suit. Liberated and educated women have left the church in droves. They have had good reason to do so.

I was very disappointed to read in the August 3-10 issue of *Christian Century* that Cardinal Joseph Bernadin of Chicago has refused to authorize the use of altar girls at liturgical services in the Chicago Archdiocese. Females are still excluded as servers at Mass. It looks as though we still have a way to go to make Paul's admonition come true: "So there is no difference . . . between men and women." (Galatians 3:28)

In our congregation we must examine our offices of ushers and Elders, Council and Sunday School teachers, to make sure we are not promoting the outrageous notion that women must bake the cookies, serve the tea and punch, and be the secretaries, while men conduct the "important business" of God's Kingdom.

In all this we must get on our knees and ask God not only for forgiveness, but for the foresight to launch out like the Bloomer Woman from Council Bluffs and make a difference.

While our Christian Church history on the issue of women is not helpful, our theology is quite clear. God's people are admonished to throw off all prejudices and bigotry; they are told that the call to be a part of the baptized family of God is all-inclusive. In the Christian Church there are no second-class citizens, no one ruling over another, no calling inferior what the Almighty has created. All people must have their human dignity before God and in any society of God's created people.

None other than sometime-chauvinistic St. Paul wrote to the Church at Galatia: "So there is no difference between Jews and Gentiles, between slaves and free people, between men and women; you are all one in union with Christ Jesus." (Galatians 3:28)

To discriminate or behave in a sexist manner toward someone merely because of their unique plumbing and reproductive system is a slap in the face of our Creator God and a heartbreak to His Son who died on a cross for us all. Certainly the Holy Spirit must cringe in disappointment as She hears the sexist and vulgar jokes and comments which promote such an attitude in our daughters and sons as they mature in the faith.

I was embarrassed and ashamed of our President's comments to the Business and Professional Women in Washington recently. The worst part was not what he said, but the fact that he thought what he said was humorous and a compliment to women. In this case, I side with Johnny Carson who said that [Our] "President . . . must have Henry VIII as his advisor on women's issues."

The trite excusing of the whole sexist attitude that dominates all of our society cannot be dismissed with hoots about "bra burners" or the likes of Phyllis Schlafly or off-hand comments like that by the President. It is one of the great issues of our day, and it's about time our Christian faith, and those who espouse it, pray through it, and come up with some effective leadership for change.

To pray, to stand, and to work for mutual respect and rights for women, is indeed Christ-like. In His ministry Jesus astounded and angered the men of His day, and, no doubt, some of the women too. He stopped to help the woman with a hemorrhage; He gave forgiveness and love to the woman at the well; He stayed with Simon Peter's mother-in-law on the nothern edge of the Sea of Galilee; He included in the inner circle Mary Magdalene; and He made His first Easter appearance not to the male

Church Council, but to two women He loved. He pointed to a widow in the Temple as the best example of stewardship.

Amelia Bloomer taught Sunday School in her Church at Council Bluffs — she was better than 130 years ahead of her time in seeing the theology of an all-inclusive God and the consistency of Christ's teaching with the right of women to vote.

Like other burning issues in society — such as peace, racism, the plight of the poor — it's not good enough to make statements against evils in the safety of our Worship Service. Disciples must get out into the world, like Amelia Bloomer did, and make a difference. We are asked by Christ to be the leaven, the salt, the light to all that affects life itself. Evil and bondage in God's creation must be confronted and called out of its demonic forms — it must be identified and named for what it really is — a perversion of God's natural and beautiful creation.

That's why I think we need to be aggressive in supporting an Equal Rights Amendment, equal pay for equal work, equal representation for equal population, and so forth. Let's not let silly, unenlightened comments like "all use the same restroom" fog over the real issues. Amelia Jenks Bloomer had it right when she talked of women's rights: "Woman has a right to vote for civil officers, to hold offices, and so to rule over men . . . Deborah ruled Israel 40 years, and, instead of being told she was out of her sphere . . . we are assured that she was highly-approved and that she ruled wisely and well . . . What was right for Deborah was right for Queen Victoria. If it is right for Victoria to sit on the throne of England, it is right for any American woman to occupy the Presidential chair at Washington. All that is needed are votes enough to elevate her to that post of honor and trust and sufficient ability to discharge its duties. Of the latter requisite, judging from some of those who have already occupied that seat, no great amount is demanded." *Life and Writings of Amelia Bloomer*, page 159.

I thrill to the way Amelia Bloomer used the same Scripture male preachers have been using to keep a hold on women and turned it around to scold them for their pulpit bigotry.

Amelia didn't continue to wear the bloomers for all her life. She found the Iowa prairies too windy for a short skirt and writes: "I was greatly annoyed and mortified by having my skirts turned over my head and shoulders on the streets — I kept the dress 'til after the introduction of hoops." *Life and Writings of Amelia Bloomer*, page 72.

She is an "Iowa Parable," an all-time great — the Bloomer Woman from Council Bluffs. We honor her today. We honor her because she is an example of taking an unpopular stand consistent with our Christian faith and making a profound difference in lives of generations which followed after her.

Amelia is buried in Fairview Cemetery high on a hill in Council Bluffs. On her monument are these words:

Amelia Jenks Bloomer
Wife of Dexter C. Bloomer
Age 76 years, 7 months, and 3 days
A pioneer in Woman's Enfranchisement.

Down the hill from her gravesite is a school named Bloomer School. I traveled there to take a picture. Ironically, however, it is named after her husband — the male Dexter Bloomer!

We have a long way yet to go so that " . . . there is no difference between Jews and Gentiles, between slaves and free people, between men and women; we are all one in union with Christ Jesus." (Galatians 3:28) Amen.

Next week we'll consider "The Hidden Treasure of Siam."

Bloomer grave site.

CHAPTER 7

The Hidden Gold of Siam

Suggested Scriptures:
Isaiah 33:1-6
James 5:1-5a
Luke 12:13-21

Suggested Hymn:
"Take My Life, that I May Be"

The "Klondike."

Our State of Iowa holds in its courthouses and historical societies a wealth of stories and parables that can illustrate very graphically how things are with us who live here, and what our God is like who watches over us. Every little village has its favorite tales that have been told and retold from one generation to another.

In these stories is the folk wisdom, the beliefs, and priorities of generations of Iowans who have gone before us. I have related to you some of the stories like:

The Little Brown Church in the Wildwood at Nashua;
Belle Plaine's Gusher;
A plough in an oak tree near Exira;
and of Iowans like:

Jesse Hiatt and his apples;
Kate Shelley and her rescue;
and last week, Amelia Jenks and her bloomers.

Today, its a mystery which includes murder, ghosts, an eccentric doctor, and buried treasure.

If you travel southeast to the Taylor County seat, Bedford, employees there in the courthouse may deny there ever was a trial held in July of 1915. But across the street from the courthouse is the Library, and there, with some persistent digging, you can find the newspaper of the day, *The Bedford Free Press*, that tells it all.

The librarian told me there are still those who read the articles and take off in jeeps for Siam to use their metal detectors and hunt for buried gold.

According to the newspaper account, in July of 1915, the streets and courthouse of Bedford were packed with people and reporters — 800 folks tried to get into Justice of the Peace Sawyer's courtroom.

Out on the gravel roads near Siam, on the farm he now owns, Philip Hardee can still show you the ridges of the earth left by the horse-drawn scoop shovels of many a treasure seeker from 1915 on for 25 years.

Today treasure seekers with metal detectors, wander across the hills of the old Bates Huntsman and Sam Anderson farms, tramping down the crops and looking for three trunks loaded with gold. So many have searched there that the nickname for the area is "The Klondike."

The story of this buried treasure of Siam varies considerably, depending on who is telling it and what newspaper account you read.

Here is the way Maria Porter told the story to a reporter of *The Free Press* and to the crowded courtroom in Bedford's courthouse in 1915, 47 years after it happened.

In 1868 a wealthy cattleman named Old Than, and a young boy, were murdered. They had come up from Missouri to sell some cattle. Their trunk of money, including gold worth about $90,000, was stolen and buried on the Bates Huntsman farm near Siam. Bates Huntsman told his neighbor, Sam Anderson, of the deed, and promised him a fourth of the treasure if he would help dig whenever he asked. He claimed the treasure map that told of the location had been burned in his cabin fire. So for 25 years they dug, often late at night by lantern light.

Neighbor Anderson related how a screaming ghost had appeared one night out of the locust grove where they were searching near the unmarked grave of the young lad who was buried there. He also claimed they had found a tin box and that Bates Huntsman pulled a gun and never did give him his promised share. If he had, the story that you hear today might never have come to light.

Not until 1914 did the 72-year-old Anderson tell his story to a lawyer by the name of W. W. Bulman in Chariton, Iowa. So in 1915, brash young Attorney Bulman set Bedford on its ear by filing suit, charging four highly-regarded Taylor County residents — Nathaniel and John Damewood, Sam Scrivner, and Bates Huntsman — with murder. He also implicated a recently-deceased eccentric Doctor Golliday, who was found dead in his drugstore bedroom with gold and cash scattered all around him.

According to a front page article in *The Bedford Free*

Press, the four accused, along with two others deceased since, hired a gang to murder the two Missourians, then dump the man's body in a well and bury the lad in the locust grove.

The loot was hidden on the Huntsman farm in three different spots, and a map was drawn showing their locations. They hunted for that treasure for nearly a quarter of a century!

On the day of the trial, Maria Collins Porter said she had seen these men, when she was a young girl of fourteen, carry a man's body through the woods. Her brother-in-law, Jonathan Dark, threatened to kill her and to "wash his hands in her heart's blood" if she ever told.

Maria claimed the men brought the bloody quilt which had been used to carry the alleged body and made her wash the red stains out of it.

Justice of the Peace Sawyer granted a defense motion to dismiss the case after the Iowa Attorney General pleaded for dismissal because there was no body, no weapon, and no treasure.

But the old-timers around Siam still claim there is a ghost in that locust grove, and that it protects a young lad's murdered body which lies there. Some would insist there is still treasure to be found in those Taylor County hills.

It's an Iowa Parable about treasure and people's search for it.

The Scriptures have a lot to say about treasures. Isaiah claims about God's people, "Their greatest treasure is their reverence for the Lord." (Isaiah 32:6b)

The brother of our Lord writes about the rich people of his day, "Your gold and silver have rusted, and their rust will be evidence against you . . . you have laid up treasure for the last days." (James 5:3)

Jesus told a parable about a rich man who was blessed with a great harvest and built bigger barns and died without enjoying them — then He concluded, "So is he who lays up treasure for himself, and is not rich toward God." (Luke 12:21)

Mrs. Porter said in *The Free Press* in 1915:

> *Now when they have all the things the world can give them, this old murder comes back to accuse them. I always knew it would. I told them God would bring it about some way and He did through the fight they got into over that cursed gold.* (Bedford Free Press, July 13, 1915)

Let's look at what this Polk Township parable has to say to us who live three generations later.

Our best treasure is our relationship to our God. Isaiah reminds us that, "Their greatest treasure is their reverence for the Lord." (Isaiah 32:6) Bates Huntsman and Sam Anderson spent 25 years of their lives hunting in the dirt for hidden wealth. It was available to them the whole time in their Christian faith. They should have looked up instead of down.

What wealth was available to those men, had they only used all that digging energy in searching the Scripture and investigating the fellowship of God's Kingdom! We can be enormously blessed and incredibly wealthy when we give up worshipping gold and start the adventure of loving and serving God and His people.

Jesus warned us that it would be impossible to worship money and God. He told His disciples, "No servant can be the slave of two masters; he will hate one and love the other; he will be loyal to one and despise the other. You cannot serve both God and money."

Jesus told those disciples that they would have to make choices in order to know the richness of being a part of God's family. So do we in our discipleship.

Who can put a dollar value on such things as:
friendships within the congregation;
the help others give when we are struggling;

the presence of God's Spirit in our lives;

the privilege of Communion and forgiveness with other sinners;

the adoption through baptism into the very daughter-and sonship of the Almighty.

And when in singing the hymns and sharing the Good News — loving each other here — what treasure God gives to us and how valuable it is to our sense of well-being, of belonging, and of high self-esteem!

Those men of Siam hunted all those years for that buried treasure, when it was already available above ground in the churches and congregations and in the beautiful sunrises and sunsets and gorgeous creation of God all around them. They had their heads in the dirt hole and could not see the God around them.

Isaiah understood when he said, "Their greatest treasure is their reverence for the Lord."

We, too, can kill for gold like those men: Scrivner, Huntsman, and the Damewood boys.

We can kill a good marriage, murder the possibility of a rewarding friendship, wipe out the development and growth of our own selves to the full creative possibility God has given us; and it can be murder at home and at work and during our leisure time if money and gold is our only end goal. Hear me well: the Scripture doesn't condemn having money, it simply says that to have money means it's a very treacherous time in our Christianity and that it's how we use and share that money that's crucial to our discipleship.

Sam Anderson did all that digging in the ground when he might have found treasure in his neighbor the next farm over. Often we kill ourselves, risk our own health, even commit a slow, or not-so-slow, suicide by sacrificing all good reason to get and keep wealth and possessions and creature comforts. Sometimes it can be a habit that the American way of life forces on us, and sometimes it's just plain greed and self-indulgence. Either way, it's murder!

Jesus told a parable about an all-consuming greed to get and keep when He told of the man who built larger and larger barns. Finally, just when he thought he had about enough and would now start to enoy it — he died. Our Lord ended His parable this way: "This is how it is with those who pile up riches for themselves but are not rich in God's sight." (Luke 12:21)

If what Mrs. Porter claims is true — then Old Than, the cattleman, and his boy, were killed because some young men wanted something for nothing. Such a hope is always an illusion and brings violence, bloodshed, and inevitably comes back to haunt us.

We can too easily get sidetracked and mired down in trying to get wealth and creature comforts for this life. Carol and I went down to the old Huntsman farm and walked through the locust grove, finding the approximate location of the well, looking at the rough spots treasure seekers left in the earth. We were crossing a little creek and Carol stepped on what looked like solid ground. In and down she went into the mire and quicksand. I laughed — and paid for it later. Phil Hardee was more diplomatic. He helped her. That's the way it can be in our treasure-seeking. If we take our eyes off the real treasure, the Christ, for just a moment, it looks like solid ground, but it quickly sucks us in and we are engulfed with the greed and priorities of the world.

The greak task and privilege of the Christian lifestyle is to locate our real treasure. It is to point out to us that which is precious to us.

We have a map that cannot burn in a cabin fire. It locates our treasure through the Scriptures and tells us of a God who loves and forgives, a Savior to whom we are precious, who treasures us, and who gave His life for us on the cross of Calvary. In that treasure map is revealed a ghost different from the one of the locust grove; it is one who is named God's presence with us here — the Holy

Spirit. There is in that Scripture a treasure cache of strength, encouragement, calm, and peace for our troubled days. We need not be haunted by guilt for our actions or be consumed by greed for gold in the ground. We have been given a completely difference set of priorities to live by and friends with which to celebrate them. Maria Porter alleged that these four men buried those trunks of gold, finally found them, and then cheated each other and fought over the wealth.

Phil A. Hardee.

Philip Hardee, who now owns the land, and whose grandfather sat in on the trial and lived in the community at the time, has a different theory about the gold. He believes there's gold there for certain, but that the gold is from the Jesse James gang who hid it next to a well and got out of there before a posse could capture them. That would make sense, as the rumor still persists in the area that Jonathan Dark was one of the men who rode with the Jesse James gang. He was Maria Porter's brother-in-law. I'm sure Sam Scrivner likes Phil Hardee's version better than the one that Attorney Bulman brought forward at the trial!

In April of 1908, there was an eccentric doctor in Bedford by the name of Alfred M. Golliday, whom a Mr. Frantz found dead in his sleeping room in the drugstore. When they began to look around, they found lots of gold and cash all over the apartment — it was hidden in cans and containers under the bed and even in the flooring. The 1915 trial brought that death and treasure to light, and some were sure the good doctor was part of the plot.

Let's consider it carefully. In the doctor's bedroom were hidden cans and containers full of gold. On the Huntsman farm is treasure buried in the ground. We have a dead doctor whose reputation is tarnished. We have six Taylor County senior citizens fighting over some alleged gold. That's the way it is with gold. It's not wrong to earn it and have it. It's how we share and use it that really counts. It's treacherous stuff to have around us as God's disciples. We cannot allow our lives to revolve around it.

Jesus said, "For your heart will always be where your riches are." (Luke 12:34)

How happy those men could have been if they had helped the poor, fed the hungry, supported the good in Bedford and Taylor County, tithed all they had to their church. Then they would have felt wealth beyond their wildest imaginations!

It's an Iowa Parable — it's about theft and treasure. It says to us that the great task and privilege of the Christian lifestyle is to locate our real treasure. Our best treasure is our relationship to God and to each other.

They tell me that late at night, around the locust grove on the old Huntsman farm, occasionally when the moon is full, you can still hear the ring of pick and shovel, and once in a while get a very brief glimpse of a ghost hovering in the tall locust trees.

It's an Iowa Parable. Amen.

Next week we will travel to Imogene, Iowa, to hear of August Werner, a cabinet builder who flew the first helicopter years before the Wright Brothers at Kittyhawk. It's also an Iowa Parable.

CHAPTER 8

August Werner
Gets Off the Ground

Suggested Scriptures:
Micah 7:14 & 7:18-20
Hebrews 4:14-5:4
Luke 6:27-36

Suggested Hymn:
"There's a Wideness in God's Mercy"

August Werner and his Flying Machine, by Larry Greenwalt.

On December 17, 1903, Wilbur and Orville Wright flew their airplane at Kittyhawk and are usually credited by most people as the "Fathers of Aviation" in this country.

Most Iowans do not know that while they lived in Iowa these two sons of Bishop Wright tried to fly long before Kittyhawk. Bishop Wright had returned from a church convention to his home in Cedar Rapids with a flying toy which resembled a helicopter and powered by a rubber band. His sons, Wilbur and Orville, built several and could get them to fly. But when they made one on a larger scale, it would not get off the ground.

After the Wright family moved from Iowa in 1881, they started to work on a fixed-wing plane which they eventually flew at Kittyhawk.

Seventeen years before the Wright brothers took off at Kittyhawk, a German immigrant, August Werner, who lived in Imogene, built and flew the world's first plane over a pasture field.

It's an Iowa Parable about the little guy, the oddball and misfit, who marches to a different drummer from the great majority of people.

It is a sad story, for unlike Amelia Bloomer and Kate Shelley, August Werner never knew he had accomplished something renowned, nor did he even think he was anything more than a failure.

Here, then, in his story:

In the 1870s and 1880s in the little town of Imogene, Iowa, lived a single woodworker by the name of August Werner. He was a religious man, a Lutheran baptized August Freder, rather quiet and introspective. Around the tiny settlement of Irish Catholics he was known for his excellent cabinet making skill — it was difficult to get something done in his shop, though, because he was always tinkering with his inventions.

One of the gadgets August made was a small, wooden model of what we would call today a helicopter. The thing could lift itself several inches off the ground with its overhead propeller.

The word got out that this eccentric woodworker was building a large model. He announced that on July 4, 1886, he would fly the world's first airplane. The day arrived, and August and some men carried the contraption to a little hill east of town, where a large crowd of curious had gathered. Most of the people scoffed at the notion that a man could actually fly in a machine.

Werner got caught up in the excitement of the moment and made some very rash and optimistic promises. He announced he would take off and have dinner with President Cleveland in Washington, and supper with the Kaiser in Berlin!

He climbed into his flying machine and peddled with all his might. The cog-wheels began to rotate the monstrous blade through a series of gears — the crowd gasped — then held their breath.

Could their peculiar Imogene woodworker actually peddle his way up through the clouds and on to Washington? They could see it start to lift off . . . then the cogs snapped — and with them Werner's dream. The first flying machine collapsed in a disheveled heap around its creator.

The cruel crowd hooted and laughed at the disappointed flyer and his wreck of a machine. He had a far piece to go to make it to Washington, D.C., for dinner with the President — he hadn't even made it out of Fremont County! They showed him no mercy with their jeering and guffawing. Werner remained on the hillside, a broken and humiliated man.

History is vague as to whether or not August Werner got off the ground.

Charles Abbot, who died not so long ago, was 21 years old at the time, and was an eyewitness. He claimed that the homemade helicopter got about four feet in the air before the cogs broke. Then it dropped to ruins. John Delehant and R. R. Armstrong, who also were there, claimed it never got off the Imogene turf.

The sad part of this Iowa story is that Werner never recovered from the humiliation of the crowd that famous Fourth of July. The next December he was admitted to the State Hospital at Clarinda. He remained there, continuing his woodworking craft for 45 years until his death in 1931. In 1907, four years after the Wright Brothers' flight and 21 years after August's committal, a Frenchman named Paul Cornu was credited with the first successful manned helicopter flight.

Werner was, either way, ahead of his time or crazy. Time has certainly proved he had a correct idea.

August Werner was the first person to build and fly an airplane. It was July 4, 1886, and it was over a pasture field at Imogene, Iowa. It's an Iowa Parable, and it has a lot to say to us about:

*Individuality — those people different from the
     mass of humanity;*
God's mercy and how we treat each other.
Our tendency to narrow God's mercy;
*And to conform, rather than transform, the
     world's standards.*

This is a parable about God's mercy and how we treat each other. Crowds can be cruel. They jeered at August Werner's attempt to fly. He was so depressed over his treatment by neighbors he nearly died. He was committed to Clainda State Hospital all those years.

There are times when we are not treated well by others. Times when our alleged friends turn on us, and when we are deeply hurt because people laugh and make light and don't even pay attention.

Some of us have experienced parents or spouses like that. No matter how well we do something, they always find fault or reason to ridicule. Many of us have co-workers or supervisors who behave in this fashion. What can be even more devastating is when we have done something, and they simply refuse to notice or to compliment in any way — there is just conspicuous silence.

At times like that we need not be depressed and give up as August Werner did. God still loves, even when we fail, when we embarrass ourselves, and when the crowds jeer and make us the butt of their cruel fun.

The author of Hebrews writes, "Our High Priest is not one who cannot feel sympathy for our weaknesses." (Hebrews 4:15)

Our God delights in loving the loser, the one defeated, the inadequate. You don't have to win to be one of God's family. He delights in us even when we are foolish and silly and make terrible, embarrassing mistakes. Micah writes, ". . . you take pleasure in showing us your constant love." (Micah 7:18b)

Now, if for no other reason, because God is so generous with us in our failures and disappointments, we must treat each other in the same sensitive, forgiving way as He treats us.

If only that Irish Catholic crowd on the Fourth of July would have been more loving and gentle with their local Lutheran inventor — aviation history might have been different. "Good show, August — let me help you rebuild and let's try again." "I don't think you'll get to Washington, D.C., Werner, but let's see if we can replace those wooden cogs and start over. We might get you over to Randolph or down to Sidney." "You got a great idea, August, keep on working at it — we're proud of you."

We have a very practical parable today about hurting people and how God wants to work through us to help soothe and heal the wounds of defeat.

When Jesus was telling the disciples about how to live

as God's people, He put it like this: "Be merciful just as your Father is merciful." (Luke 6:36) August could have used some of that mercy!

It's also a parable about our tendency to narrow God's mercy. The people of Imogene made fun of August because he wasn't quite like them. He ended up committed to the mental institution at Clarinda. That's where and when we still often put people different from ourselves. We have a tendency to lock the different and unlovely out of our sight. They make us uncomfortable.

When we use such words as "welfare cheats" and "unemployed sponges," we're violating what the New Testament Christ told His disciples: "If you love only the people who love you, why should you receive a blessing? Even sinners love those who love them!" (Luke 6:32)

Christian discipleship involves a very radical love. It involves a love for those different from us. It involves one not returned or deserved or easily given.

We have the compassion of the loving Father for the prodigal. Our lives are to be like what Jesus demonstrated around Galilee and down toward Jericho. He loved:

the wretched poor,
the beggars and lepers,
the social outcasts,
those who stink and cheat,
even those who curse and deny the Almighty.

Jesus gave His life on a cross for such as those, also, and we must have His love for them.

The real temptation of a congregation is to accept only, and invite exclusively, those people just like us. I mean those of white, middle-class, European background, who dress about the same way we dress. That is to narrow God's mercy. That is a violation of how God is and how we are to treat each other.

Back in about 1855, Frederick W. Faber wrote:

*There's a wideness in God's mercy, Like the
    wideness of the sea;*
*There's a kindness in his justice Which is more
    than liberty.*
*There is no place where earth's sorrows Are more
    felt than up in heav'n.*
*There is no place where earth's failings Have such
    kindly judgment giv'n.* (#290, LBW)

This is also a parable about our conforming to the world's ways. August Werner was odd. He was different. He marched to a different beat. And most geniuses do! People with great vision, those with brilliant insight, are often different. We ought not ridicule them for it, but support their individuality and celebrate their unique, god-given gifts.

To my dying day I'll regret how I used to help a group of boys on Saturday night in the little town of Greenville when I was growing up. We came in to Greenville on a Saturday night to park our car along main street and watch the people walk by. There was a hearing-impaired man who was nicknamed "Dummy" Parker. We boys used to tease him and watch his reactions. He wasn't like us, so we had to make fun. I recall how he would look like he was enjoying all the attention, but I now know his heart must have ached because of the lack of love from us.

We must be careful how we educate our children and treat people around us who just don't fit the mold. Let's refrain from trying to make everyone be like us. There ought to be room for the different. He or she, too, is a product of God's creation, and one for whom Christ died. The hyperkinetic, the blind, the hearing-impaired, the retarded, the genius, the quiet, the musical, the shy, the ones whose sexual preference is different from ours, the bookworm, the long-hair and the short-hair and the no-hair; also, the crazy who built a wooden airplane. We need see all of these as God's family we are to love and include.

The world will try to put us all in neat little compartments. However, we are not to conform to the world's standards; but rather, work for change and transformation of them into God's Kingdom standards.

Jesus taught this and turned upside-down the priorities of His day when He said, "Happy are you poor and you hungry and you who weep. "Happy are you when people reject you and insult you. Be glad when that happens and dance for joy." (Luke 6:20-23)

When the God-man Jesus came to earth, the crowds didn't treat Him very well, either. He came back to His hometown and they ran Him out of the synagogue and tried to stone Him. Now people travel from all over the world just to try to find that particular sysnagogue.

He didn't order his life by the same priorities and the crowds couldn't understand. So they killed Him on Calvary. The surprise is that that crucifixion on Calvary made the crucified's way be held up before the world from then on. It gave, and still gives, solace to the person who is different and teaches the rest of us how to treat each other — with the love and acceptance of God Himself.

It's quite a parable from Imogene, Iowa. It wasn't until 1912, 26 years later, that Iowan Billy Robinson of Grinnell flew at the Iowa State Fair — the next Iowan to get off the ground. His community got behind him, even when his first rotary engine blew up and he had to start over. They formed the Grinnell Aeroplane Company and continued to accept Billy until he died in his plane crash south of town.

But credit for the first attempt belongs to a German immigrant from Imogene, whom the crowd jeered and made fun of, August Werner.

His story is a parable about our conforming to the world's standards instead of celebrating our different gifts. It's also a parable about our tendency to narrow God's wide mercy, and it's a parable about a merciful God and how we treat each other.

August Werner grave site.

August died "intestate" at Clarinda August 28, 1931. His obituary in the *Evening Sentinel* of Shenandoah was three sentences long:

> *August Warner [sic], formerly of here was buried from the M.E. church here Friday afternoon. Mr. Werner was found dead in bed at his home in Clarinda where he has lived the last 30 years. Rev. Shurman of Strahan conducted the funeral.*

I've driven out the dirt road to the Old German Lutheran Memorial Cemetery, which lies northeast of Imogene, to see his grave marker. It has on it a very simple inscription:

August Werner
1849-1931

Even in death Werner was different. All the tombstones in that cemetery face the east . . . except for inventor August's . . . it faces west. Still, I wonder who was really out of step?

Next week, we'll look at the Cardiff Giant, which was America's greatest hoax. Amen.

CHAPTER 9

The Giant From Fort Dodge's Gypsum

Suggested Scriptures:
Genesis 6:1-8
James 1:22-27
Luke 18:9-14

Suggested Hymn:
"Christ Is Alive! Let Christians Sing"

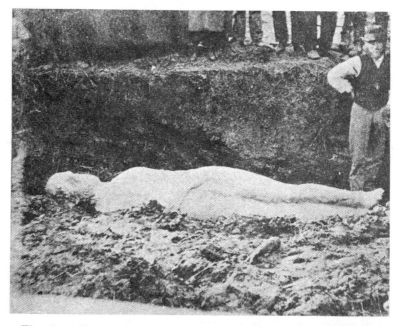

The Cardiff Giant, from New York State Historical Association.

This summer we have looked at the tales of Iowa and Iowans that are told with such delight in small-town barber shops, courthouses, beauty salons, filling stations, across backyard fences, and in country club locker rooms.

It's been fun . . . I have delighted in the vast variety of religious truths that have been illustrated by these Iowa Parables, such as:

August Werner and his Flying Machine;

The Hidden Treasure of Siam;

The Bloomer Girl of Council Bluffs;

Belle Plaine's Gusher;

The Plough in the Tree;

Jesse Hiatt and his Apples;

The Little Brown Church in Wildwood;

and, Kate Shelley, Boone County Heroine.

Today let's look at what is probably Iowa's best-known and most-told story: "The Cardiff Giant."*

It has a lot to say to us about how foolish we can be arguing over Old Testament giants when we have 20th century monsters to battle. It warns us about genuine and false religion. And it reminds us how different our God is who came out of the grave to be with us here.

It's been called the "great American hoax," and it began in the little Methodist church of the northeastern Iowa town of Ackley.

It was 1866, and a Reverend Turk preached a revival sermon based on Genesis 6:4, which talked about giants. The Scripture text reads, "In those days, and even later, there were giants on the earth who were descendants of human women and the supernatural beings."

Seated in the congregation that day was a seller of

---

*Much of the information about the Cardiff Giant in this parable was obtained from a booklet by Barbara Franco, published by the New York State Historical Association, entitled *The Cardiff Giant, A Hundred-Year-Old Hoax.*

cigars, George Hull, a confirmed scoundrel, who even looked the part of a villain with black hair, mustache and beard, and dressed in black from his boot toes to his plug hat. He was an atheist, an inveterate rogue, and a man of talent and imagination.

After hearing the sermon on giants, Hull wondered if people would really believe in them. So in June of 1868 he and a partner, H. B. Martin, went to Fort Dodge to the gypsum quarries to obtain a piece large enough for a giant. The block measured 12' x 4' x 22". They shipped the gypsum block to Chicago, where a marble cutter, Edward Burghardt, had it fashioned into the likeness of a statue. Hull stayed with the clandestine project, and some think it was carved after *his* likeness.

At first the giant had hair and a beard, but then Hull discovered these do not petrify, so he had them chipped away. The thing was given an ancient appearance by washing it with sulfuric acid and then rubbing it with sand.

When the work was complete, the gypsum giant was shipped to Cardiff, New York, by a circuitous route. At midnight on November 9, the wagon carrying the giant arrived at the farm of Hull's relative, Stub Newell. There it was buried five feet underground.

After nearly a year, in 1869, according to plan, men were hired to dig a well right where the giant had been entombed. October 16, to their surprise, the innocent welldiggers unearthed the body of a "prehistoric man."

People began to gather as the gypsum giant was gradually revealed. The career of the Cardiff Giant had begun.

By Monday morning, farmer Newell had erected barriers and was charging 50 cents apiece to see the giant. By midweek Newell's farm had been completely transformed to accommodate the curious. The crowds started to arrive. They overran the place.

Stages ran to and from Cardiff from Syracuse every day. The visitors would pay their 50 cents, go into the little dark tent, and peer in awe-struck silence at this great discovery still lying in the hole where it was unearthed.

People were eager to see the giant; Newell and his neighbors were eager to make money from the alleged find. The hotel at Cardiff hadn't done such business in years! Neighboring farms rented rooms and sold cider, meals, oysters, and even oats for the horses.

A little later the former mayor of Syracuse got wind that P. T. Barnum was trying to buy the giant, so he and three other respected businessmen bought three-quarter interests for $30,000 and relocated it in their city. As the giant was raised from its grave, the state geologist was on hand to examine its underside. The New York Central Railroad made special arrangements for a ten-minute stop so passengers could view the relocated spectacle.

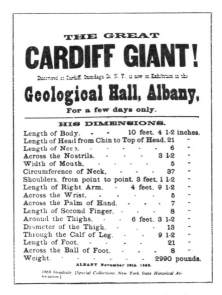

Advertisement for Cardiff Giant
from New York State Historical Association, Cooperstown, N.Y.

In the New York elections that fall, the Cardiff Giant received votes for a number of state offices.

One day a lawyer from Fort Dodge by the name of Gahusha Parsons started to investigate. He discovered the entire hoax. About the same time a young paleontologist at Yale University published his opinion: "It is of very recent origin and a decided humbug."

Hull, anxious to show how he had flim-flammed the gullible public, told the whole story. Some still insisted on believing. Finally, when the two sculptors from Chicago admitted they had carved the thing, the giant's popularity declined. America's greatest hoax was exposed for what it really was — a hunk of gypsum from Fort Dodge, Iowa.

It's one of Iowa's famous stories. It's one of God's parables.

Let's see what it has to say to us this year.

It's foolish to argue about Old Testament giants when we have so many 20th-century monsters to battle. A century ago, Americans would travel for miles to visit this alleged prehistoric giant and not see the monsters on all sides of them.

One of the hazards for Christians and in telling these "Iowa Parables," is that we try to escape into the past with great reverence and so ignore that which is unpleasant and cruel and needs to be changed in the present.

Genesis 6:4 says there were giants on the land. It's just plain foolish for us to debate and hang our faith on such silly issues as to whether or not there were demons — giants. We mustn't argue over whether there was a devil and a snake and a tree, or an ark on the flooded earth or a whale which swallowed a man. Let's take these stories as we have taken our Iowa Parables and see what God is saying through them to us in our time. Let's consider what those inspired writers wanted to reveal about God's truth to us.

Certainly it's the day for biblical literalists and conservative and liberal and Baptist, Lutheran, Roman Catholic, and all sorts and kinds of Christians, to join hands and work together, that we might battle those monsters that so threaten humankind now.

There is the monster of greed. Look how it gnaws away at the very fabric of our society! We seem to have entered into the '80s with a renewed lust for having and getting and keeping for ourselves. Christians seem to justify almost any behavior if it makes money. That is a monster we need to fight.

It wasn't right for Stub Newell and George Hull to charge 50 cents to see their giant — it was plain dishonesty. Honesty is a virtue that again needs to be held up as good and right in our day.

A second monster of our day is hunger. There are so many in the world, and their number is increasing, who are starving while the farmers of our land are paid not to grow crops. Starvation, malnutrition — these things are everyday guests in millions of homes, while many people throughout the world will live their whole lives hungry.

Pastor Moses Mwakisimba of Tanzania, East Africa, who spent last December with us here at this church, writes the following: "We regretted to let you know that in our country we don't have food. Clothes, soaps, sugar, salt, and other very important things. We are very poor. We suffer a lot. We have to pay much money to Uganda and Japan — because of war between Uganda and Tanzania we had long ago."

We have the monster of racism and sexism still in our day. It tries to devour us. It keeps us from being the loving fellowship we are created to be. It prevents our family of God from reaching its full potential as a caring people.

A decade ago there was a great civil rights march in Washington, D.C., and there was a greater address by Martin Luther King, Jr., when he announced he had a dream. We have a long way yet to go to realize that dream. We have a long way yet to go to realize the dream God had for us when He created us and put us in this Eden.

Hate instead of love still wins in our society. Bigotry instead of inclusiveness still takes the day, rules the majority, and is present within our congregation.

The giant of militarism is another monster we need to conquer. It sends the Marines instead of the Peace Corps. It talks of more and more weapons and tools of human destruction instead of reason and negotiation.

You see, we can't afford the luxury of debating about giants on the earth of the Old Testament when we have so many demonic monsters attacking our humanity and nipping at our heels from all sides right now.

This Iowa story is also a parable about genuine and false religion. George Hull and Stub Newell fooled the public with their phony giant. It was close enough to the real thing to make it almost believable.

Discipleship is like that — we can have the appearance of genuineness, but not have it really! James, the brother of our Lord, said, "What God the Father considers to be pure and genuine religion is this: to take care of orphans, widows and widowers in their suffering, and to keep oneself from being corrupted by the world." (James 1:26-27)

So our discipleship cannot just be spectatorship; it involves making a difference in the lives of people who need and hurt and suffer. It involves growing in the grace of God which was given to us at our baptism and is continually supplied to us when we don't really deserve it.

Mahatma Ghandi, who was the leader of millions in India, studied Christianity when in England, but rejected it because he saw that Christians don't live up to the teachings of Jesus.

Here in America a young Chinese studied for four years and was graduated from one of our colleges. The churches did not invite him to attend, and many people ridiculed him. He went back to China, bitter against Christianity, and became Prime Minister of Communist China.

Remember the Gospel story about the Publican and the Pharisee: the one who thought he was religious, *wasn't!* We are like the Pharisee. We who belong to the Church, and we who use religion to congratulate ourselves on how good we are, often see the Church as a gathering of fine people. Not so, said Jesus when He was preaching His series of parables: "I tell you," he said, "the tax collector, and not the Pharisee, was in the right with God when he went home." (Luke 18:14)

The tax collector approached God in fear and humility, knowing he wasn't worthy. "God, have pity on me, a sinner." (Verse 13)

The Cardiff Giant was one of America's greatest hoaxes — but the Christian Church — our baptism, and our discipleship — can also be a hoax. If we refuse to witness, to learn, to serve, to give ourselves away, and to develop and progress in our spiritual life — we, too, are as phony as that gypsum giant foisted on the public by George Hull.

There are all around us cults and organizations which try to look like the Body of Jesus Christ, but are really constructed to bilk and manipulate the people.

P. T. Barnum saw a good thing in the Cardiff Giant and tried to buy it. When he could not purchase it, he had one constructed like it and hauled it around the country, selling tickets to get in to see it. A recently sculptured replica now lies at rest at the Fort Museum in Fort Dodge, Iowa. There are movements which try to mimic the Christian faith that are much like that giant.

The Mormons, Moon's Unification Church, The Way, Hare Krishna, and others, are not the risen Body of Christ, but a person-made body that hoodwinks and flimflams gullible and often young enthusiastic love-seekers. They are a decided humbug. They are the Cardiff Giants of this year. They are a great hoax on the American people.

Our God is real, for He came out of the grave. The

proof of that is that He is with us here. We meet Him when we come to church. We see Him in other people.

The Cardiff Giant from Fort Dodge's gypsum just lies lifeless in one spot — you know it's a hoax.

After it was revealed a hoax — it was stored in a barn in Fitchburg, Massachusetts. It was then owned by a group of Fort Dodge citizens for a brief time. Then Gardner Cowles of Des Moines' Register and Tribune owned it — it was displayed at the Iowa State Fair. Now it lies in the Farmer's Museum at Cooperstown, New York.

Our god is no hoax. He is real. We meet Him face-to-face here and in our daily routine. His spirit joins us. He does not lie dead and lifeless to be moved from one museum to another like some sort of freak.

He put on human flesh and has felt the feelings we have felt, and knows what it is to hurt, to love, to celebrate, and to grieve.

When we come to worship today, it is not in a museum where we give our offerings for admission as spectators of a sideshow and peer at a freakish thing we cannot understand or with which we cannot communicate. No cold gypsum block here. We are resurrection people, we are God-alive folks, we are the Easter gathering. Our God is alive, with heartbeat and empathy, compassion and love.

We come here to enjoy His love, loving Him and one other. There is a feeling and aliveness in this giant and He makes a difference in how we are and how we treat each other. We don't put limits on His body or locate it in just one place, either. I can come down this communion rail and assure you that into your hands is placed a part of the Body of Christ which you can eat and thereby know His real presence.

It's an Iowa Parable: "The Cardiff Giant from Fort Dodge's Gypsum." It makes clear to us how different our god is who came out of the grave and is with us today. It warns us about genuine and false religion. It tells us how foolish we can be arguing about Old Testament giants, when there are 20th-century monsters to battle.

It all started with a huckster by the name of George Hull who heard a sermon in Ackley, Iowa, by Reverend Turk at the Methodist church. The text was from Genesis 6:4, "In those days, and even later, there were giants on the earth . . ." Amen.

CHAPTER 10

The Hobos Come Home To Britt

A Communion Sermon

Suggested Scriptures:
Hosea 14:4-8
Acts 2:41-47
Luke 14:7-14

Suggested Hymn:
"At the Lamb's High Feast We Sing"

Britt Corporation Sign.

In August of 1900 more than 250 hobos, tramps, and "freeloaders," came by train to the little northwest Iowa town of Britt for their first annual National Hobo Convention. They ate free food, drank free beer, stayed in free accommodations, played games, drew up a political platform and nominated a candidate for the 1900 Presidential election.

Ever since then that Hancock County town has been known as "hobo haven." Better than three-quarters of a century later, the people of Britt, Iowa, are still hosting the annual National Convention of Hobos each August.

It's an Iowa story. It all began like this: A Britt resident and businessman, T. A. Potter, read in a Chicago newspaper about a number of hobos who had gathered at Danville, Illinois, for a meeting. Potter wrote to the secretary of the organizaton and showed the article to the local newspaper editor, E. M. Bailey.

The two approached the representative of the organization, "Big Brother" Charles F. Noe, and promised a carload of beer and free food for two days to all the group who would meet at Britt. Mr. Noe and "Onion" Cotton, "head pipe" of the group, accepted the offer and August 22, 1900, was set for the big confab.

Some have claimed this was the first national convention of any kind in Iowa — the state still doesn't do much boasting about that dubious historical fact!

Newspapers picked up the unusual event and spread the word across the nation. Reporters and all sorts of people from far and near flocked to the little village. Tramps came by rail from all over and trains unloaded their freight of freeloaders riding the rails every time they slowed for the Britt grade and depot. The town was decorated with tin cans and other items. The 250 guests were taken to the fairgrounds for their temporary lodging.

The first hobo convention in America was soon in session! They quickly went on record as opposing then-President McKinley because he "believed in giving work to every man."

A political platform was drawn up:

1. *All bulldogs shall be muzzled.*
2. *No baths shall be allowed for anyone.*
3. *Free and unlimited distribution of beer.*
4. *No housewife shall offer any hobo mince pie of her own making. (Tell a Tale of Iowa,* by Don Brown)

Nebuchadnezzar Lloyd of Utah made a rousing nominating speech for Admiral Dewey for President of the United States because "he never did have a home either." Dewey was nominated unanimously — something he found terribly embarrassing. Newspapers around the country published cartoons of the nomination.

Hobos on boxcar at Britt.

After a couple days, the hobos hit the rails and were gone as quickly and quietly as they had arrived. The townspeople offered to house the convention again the next year, and have been doing so ever since that August 22 of 1900. It's when the hobos come to Britt. And it's an Iowa Parable.

It can describe how our free meal, Holy Communion, really is, and how God, the host, is. It describes us undeserving children who freeload around His Table. It's also a parable about our fellowship with each other. Let's see what it can teach us.

Like those Britt hobos of 1900 who drew up their platform, you and I could also say we, too, have a platform. We who come to freeload and celebrate here with our fellowship meal called "Communion" might write our platform this way:

1. Not something we earn, but something we celebrate.
2. Not because we are worthy, but because we are loved.
3. Not proud, but thankful.
4. We eat and drink not to receive, but because we have already been given.
5. We are not perfect, but forgiven.

The hobos of Britt talked of mince pie and bulldogs in their platform — that's trite compared with what we have to sing about today when we come to this communion rail of fellowship and celebration.

It's not something we earn, but something we celebrate. The tramps invited to Britt for their big weekend hadn't done anything at all to deserve this kind of treatment. They got their special free food and drink because they were hobos. It's true when you and I come forward for this bread and wine, too. God has set this Table and paid the price that makes the menu so special.

Like hobos who come to Britt and have cheated, sworn, been lazy and ornery, so we gather here. It's

God's victory we celebrate today, not our own. He is the one who came in flesh at Bethlehem; He is the one who got disciples together around Galilee; He is the one who taught love of God and each other; He is the one who healed and ministered; He went to the cross for us; He got the family together in the upper room; He came out of the grave; and He is the one who is with us now.

It's *His* victory we observe and rejoice in. We celebrate *whose* we are, rather than *how* we are, when we gather for this good food and drink and fellowship.

It's not because we are worthy, but because we are loved. In our Gospel, Jesus tells a host: "When you give a feast, invite the poor, the crippled, the lame, and the blind; and you will be blessed, because they are not able to pay you back." (Luke 14:13)

The Scripture is full of parables which our Lord told to illustrate this principle — we are invited because we are loved, and not because we are worthy:

the banquet the loving father gave the prodigal son when he returned;

the celebration in heaven when the lost sheep was found and brought safely to the fold;

the rejoicing of the angels when the lost coin was found by the woman;

[and last Sunday we learned of the Publican being put right with God after church instead of the Pharisee].

This, then, is a grace banquet. Like Britt's hobos, God loves and invites and accepts us into the fellowship of the saved. All sorts of conventions happen *every week* and weekend in Iowa. But the hobos at Britt are different — they don't deserve it at all! They haven't worked, they are lazy, crude, dirty, dishonest, and perhaps even criminal. God sets the same kind of free banquet for us. It's the grandest demonstration of how God is. He loves us when we turn on Him, ignore Him, curse Him, use Him, take advantage of Him, and even when we are unkind to each other. He loves us when we let hate and greed and racism and hunger for power rule us. While it breaks His heart, He is still there loving, forgiving, and inviting us back home again, just like the hobos at Britt.

Hosea 14 records this promise about our God: "The Lord says, 'I will bring my people back to me. I will love them with all my heart; no longer am I angry with them. . . . . Like an evergreen tree I will shelter them; I am the source of all their blessings.' " (Hosea 14:4, 8b.)

It seems the proper place to celebrate the fact we are loved by someone. Consider how we gather around a meal table for a date, a meeting of a good friend for lunch, an observance of a wedding anniversary at a candlelit table, a wedding reception to celebrate a marriage, and a party for a birthday observance. There are graduation banquets, victory banquets, engagement banquets, Thanksgiving and Christmas banquets.

When life means most — when we want to observe how loved we are — we often gather for food and drink at table.

Only in Almighty God's eyes are we worthy to get together and celebrate this eternal undeserved love. Our platform ought to say: Not because we are worthy, but because we are loved. And it's really great to be loved!

Those Britt hobos probably get arrested in freight yards and under municipal bridges; they are thrown in county drunktanks, chased out of public parks, rousted for vagrancy, and arrested on suspicious behavior charges in other places. But in Britt, for one weekend, the roustabouts are kings and celebrate their humanity. If only for a brief time they are loved, so also are we at this table set for us in this church.

We are not proud, but thankful. Jesus promised, "For everyone who makes himself great will be humbled, and everyone who humbles himself will be made great." (Luke 14:11)

When we come forward for our banquet and join

others at the table, we don't have anything to be proud about at all. Our attitude is appreciation and not pride. If we could approach all our church attendance, our discipleship, our service and criticism, our stewardship and relationship within the Church, in this fashion, what a difference it would make in our congregation!

> *"How wonderful" instead of "I don't like that."*
> *"How can I help?" instead of "I didn't get anything out of it."*
> *"How tremendous that I'm accepted" instead of I wasn't treated well."*
> *and, "A tithe just doesn't seem like enough." instead of "Always asking for my money."*

It's recorded by St. Luke in the Book of Acts how "they spent their time in learning from the apostles, taking part in the fellowship, and sharing in the fellowship meals and the prayers." — Acts 2:42.

Then Luke tells us about those early believers: "And they had their meals together in their homes, eating with glad and humble hearts, praising God and enjoying the good will of all the people." (Acts 2:46-47)

Watch any church grow where its membership attends out of a deep sense of appreciation, rather than pride of how great they are. Watch any pastor or staff person grow and develop into a spiritual beacon when their congregation approaches them with appreciation, rather than demands and continual criticism. Luke concludes about those first Christian Church members: "And every day the Lord added to their group those who were being saved." (Acts 2:47)

We eat and drink not to receive, but because we have already been given. The hobos eat and drink at Britt because they are hobos and are celebrating that fact. It is their common bond. It is the unifying basis of their fellowship.

We come here and eat and drink because we are part of God's family. Like the family of hobos who get together at Britt, so we get together [at St. John's]. Notice this: This bread and wine is not a medicine. We do not take it to have it cure our sins. We take it because our sins *have* been forgiven. We are celebrating what already has been done for us — forgiveness, salvation, and His presence here and now to see us through this tough life.

When Jesus was about to leave the disciples on Maundy Thursday, He knew they would need Him every so often to get encouraged, inspired, filled full of His Spirit — to be reassured that He was really with them. He does the same for us.

We are not perfect, but forgiven. That's what ought be written on our foreheads as we come into our church and as we come forward to eat and drink together. Here is a celebration of the imperfect — those who make mistakes, stray from the straight and narrow, foul up relationships, offend, tramp on toes, blow the whole thing.

Like those tramp misfits who come to Britt, forgiven and accepted for a few days, so we come here for our nourishment for renewed life and strength. The Bible assures us over and over again that we need not be perfect. But, we need be sorry. Then God says to us to come on home and eat with Him as part of His forgiven family.

It's an Iowa Parable — when all the nation's bums and hobos were invited to little Britt, Iowa, and for a couple days were "knights of the road" instead of the country's freeloaders.

According to the *Des Moines Register,*

Some 20,000 people are expected at Britt this year for the annual National Hobo Convention. The Friday and Saturday Event will feature a flea market, a rock concert, midway rides, and a sky-

diving show. Highlights will be a free bowl of Mulligan Stew for visitors and the coronation of a queen and king of the hobos at 1:30 p.m. Saturday!

You and I, as God's people, also have a banquet prepared for us, and it's not for the perfect, but for the forgiven. We eat and drink not to receive, but because we have already been given. We are not proud, but thankful. We come not because we are worthy, but because we are loved. So like the annual Hobo Convention in August when the bums come home to Britt, it is not something we have earned, but something we together celebrate. And it's a parable about a merciful God and how we treat each other. Amen.

CHAPTER 11

Delhi's Unknown Poet

Suggested Scriptures:
Job 19:23-27a
1 Corinthians 15:51-57
John 12:23-26

Suggested Hymn:
"O God, Our Help in Ages Past"

Marker of Delhi Poet.

Twenty-eight-year-old John McCreery wrote a poem
back in 1863 which became famous around the world,

and for which he never received credit as author. He was on his way home late one night, depressed over the financial condition of his little newspaper — *The Delaware County Journal*. The young editor sat in his buggy behind an old horse and watched the stars as he penned those now-famous words:

"There is no death! The stars go down
To rise upon some other shore
And bright in heaven's jeweled crown
They shine for evermore."

The nine stanzas of that poem fell into place so that when he reached Delhi and his newspaper office, he immediately wrote them down and placed them in a desk drawer. What happened after that is one of Iowa's saddest stories. Eventually John Luckey McCreery was to go to his grave after 30 years of ridicule, criticism, and disillusionment. He had written a poem which would be recited beside caskets, at funerals, and in cemeteries all over the globe — but another would get the credit for it. It's an Iowa Parable.

It seems to have happened like this: McCreery sent the poem to *Arthur's Home Magazine*, a well-read booklet of the day. It was published in July of 1863. Author and publisher McCreery reprinted it in his own newspaper, as did a number of other weeklies. In fact, Eugene Bulmer of Dixon, Illinois, saw it in his local paper and included it in an article he was writing on immortality for the *Farmer's Advocate* of Chicago, Illinois. Bulmer signed his own name to the work. It gets more confusing!

Another paper saw the poem signed by Bulmer and thought it was a mistake, thus giving credit to a famous English poet by the name of F. Bulwar, Lord of Lytton. You can still find many copies of the poem with this author listed.

Our poet of Delhi was forgotten altogether. He lost his newspaper through financial ruin and moved to Dubuque. He suffered the humiliation of often seeing his poem and watching it become more and more popular, but credited to another author. Some have claimed that there isn't any other poem in the English language which has been used so often above an open grave.

McCreery tried his best to be recognized as the poem's author. He wrote letters by the hundreds claiming his authorship, but to no avail.

In 1868, the height of insult came when he actually lost a job because of this poem he wrote, but for which no one would give him credit. President Ulysses S. Grant was interviewing McCreery for the position of White House Stenographer. He seemed ready to give him the position, when someone pulled out this poem and showed it to Grant. President Grant turned down McCreery for the job because he thought, while it was a good poem, poets probably were too impractical to be good secretaries.

Well, that's the way our Delhi poet's life continued. It was miserable. He moved to Washington and served as a stenographer for the Committee on Indian Affairs.

His greatest success in claiming his poem came in 1875 when Harper Brothers listed McCreery as the poem's author in a school reader. In 1883 he released a collection of verses called "Songs of Toil and Triumph."

The unfortunate man never did receive acclaim during his lifetime for the poem "There Is No Death," and he died in 1906 in Duluth, Minnesota. He is buried in Washington, D.C.

When he died, *The Delaware County Journal,* which he once owned in the little northeast town of Delhi, Iowa, gave him about four lines for an obituary.

It's an Iowa Parable about life, about death, and about one poet's view of immortality.

This parable certainly tells us that God's people do more than provide for themselves. Mr. McCreery wrote these words the night before he died: "My only regret is that all the great work I have always contemplated doing for humanity remains undone. The bread and butter necessities of life have prevented my getting to it."

How sad — and yet how very much it is the same for us. Let's be careful lest all our life's energy is used for supporting an artificial lifestyle, and we thus fail to ever make a significant contribution to humankind.

It is easy to get mired down in supporting and satisfying ourselves and our dependents — we then never know the deep satisfaction of contributing to the basic good of other people. We certainly must provide for the "bread and butter necessities of life," but must not let the world foist on us all that additional stuff that are not necessities, and thus can take up all of our life's energies.

A correct view of life beyond the grave, which McCreery seemed to have, ought to motivate us to live differently here and now. Out of the security of our next life, we ought to be able to improve and make a difference in other lives in their world.

Since it is true that God considers us precious and has cared about us so much as to provide for us beyond the grave, and has given to us here a beautiful creation in which to live and enjoy; then, let's write the poem, the music, the check, the note of praise, that shows proper response. God has equipped us with various gifts, and we must not hoard them to ourselves or fail to develop those gifts because of our daily struggle to exist. We need not worry about getting the credit, either, like John McCreery did his whole life. With all that God has done and does give to us, it is a great satisfaction to know we have pleased our Creator God. We live by God's grace, and thus ought to be grace-full toward other people. Christian discipleship takes its satisfaction from being faithful, rather than from the accolades of the world.

St. Paul ends the great passage of Scripture about our gift of eternal life like this: "So then, my dear freinds, stand firm and steady. Keep busy always in your work for the Lord, since you know that nothing you do in the

Lord's service is ever useless." (1 Corinthians 15:58)

What sad words author McCreery wrote that eve of his death — perhaps his never getting recognition for the poem had made him a bitter person. Anyway, it's a warning to us as he writes, "My only regret is that all this great work I have always contemplated doing for humanity remains undone." Let that not be said of us.

Let's examine this Delhi poet's belief about life and death:

There is no death! The leaves may fall,
The flowers may fade and pass away —
They only wait, through wintry hours,
The coming of the May.

McCreery saw a divine plan in the universe as he rode along the Delaware County road near Delhi on that starlit night.

It seems to be the very nature of all creation, not to die, but to resurrect — we observe a cycle:

dust to flowers;

granite to leaves;

leaves to new trees;

death to new life.

Jesus spoke of the same phenomenon . . . "Unless a grain of wheat falls into the earth and dies, it remains alone; but if it dies, it bears much fruit." (John 12:23)

But how can the poet claim there is no death? Illness or disaster or old age does get us, and we're all aware of that. We all die sometime, don't we?

The point of this poet is that out of this earthly life's death, a new life is given. Just as all God's creation goes on, so do we. It's not that we got something whichGod can't kill. It's that we have an unkillable relationship with our Almighty. We have been baptized into Christ, and you can't kill that. It continues right on into eternal life.

Jesus is recorded by John as promising, "I am the resurrection and the life . . . he who believes in me, though he die, yet shall he live, and whoever lives and believes in me shall never die." (John 11:25-26a)

The poem argues that all God's creation testifies to this kind of immortality.

There is no death! The dust we tread
Shall change beneath the summer showers
To golden grain or mellow fruit
Or rainbow-tinted flowers.

Not immortal, mind you, in the sense that we are not indestructible or infinite or immortal. We are finite and mortal as humans. But immortal because of what God is and because we are joined to Him.

St. Paul assures us that, "For what is mortal must be changed into what is immortal; what will die must be changed into what cannot die. So when this takes place, and the mortal has been changed into the immortal, then the Scripture will come true: 'Death is destroyed; victory is complete.' " (1 Corinthians 15:53-54)

Our joy this day is not that we are indestructible, but that we have a loving God who won't let go, who will not desert us, who turns even that which seems like disaster in this world to victory and triumph in His eternal Kingdom.

Somehow, John McCreery, on that night long ago, sensed it and wrote it down to assure us of its validity and comfort.

The bird-like voice, whose joyous tones
Made glad this scene of sin and strife,
Sings now an everlasting song
Amid the tree of life.

There is a rock on a little grassy knoll along the seldom-used highway at the outskirts of Delhi, Iowa. On it is a bronze plaque that marks the site of John

McCreery's home and which tells of his writing the now-famous poem, "There Is No Death."

Though the poet of Delhi died, his poem lives on and has become immortal — it's one of Iowa's Parables.

It tells of a life beyond earthly life, and about how we ought, right now, to busy ourselves with things eternal.

And ever near us, though unseen,
The dear immortal spirits tread;
For all the boundless universe
Is life — there are no dead!

Amen.

There Is No Death
John Luckey McCreery

There is no death! The stars go down
To rise upon some other shore
And bright in heaven's jeweled crown
They shine for evermore.

There is no death! The dust we tread
Shall change beneath the summer showers
To golden grain or mellow fruit
Or rainbow-tinted flowers.

The granite rocks disorganize
To feed the hungry moss they bear;
The forest leaves drink daily life
From out the viewless air.

There is no death! The leaves may fall,
The flowers may fade and pass away —
They only wait, through wintry hours,
The coming of the May.

There is no death! An angel form
　　Walks o'er the earth with silent tread;
He bears our best-loved things away
　　And then we call them "dead."

He leaves our hearts all desolate —
　　He plucks our fairest, sweetest flowers;
Transplanted into bliss, they now
　　Adorn immortal bowers.

The bird-like voice, whose joyous tones
　　Made glad this scene of sin and strife,
Sings now an everlasting song
　　Amid the tree of life.

Where'er He sees a smile too bright,
　　Or soul too pure for taint or vice,
He bears it to that world of light,
　　To dwell in Paradise.

Born unto that undying life,
　　They leave us but to come again;
With joy we welcome them — the same
　　Except in sin and pain.

And ever near us, though unseen,
　　The dear immortal spirits tread;
For all the boundless universe
　　Is life — there are no dead!

Used by permission.